MAURITANIA

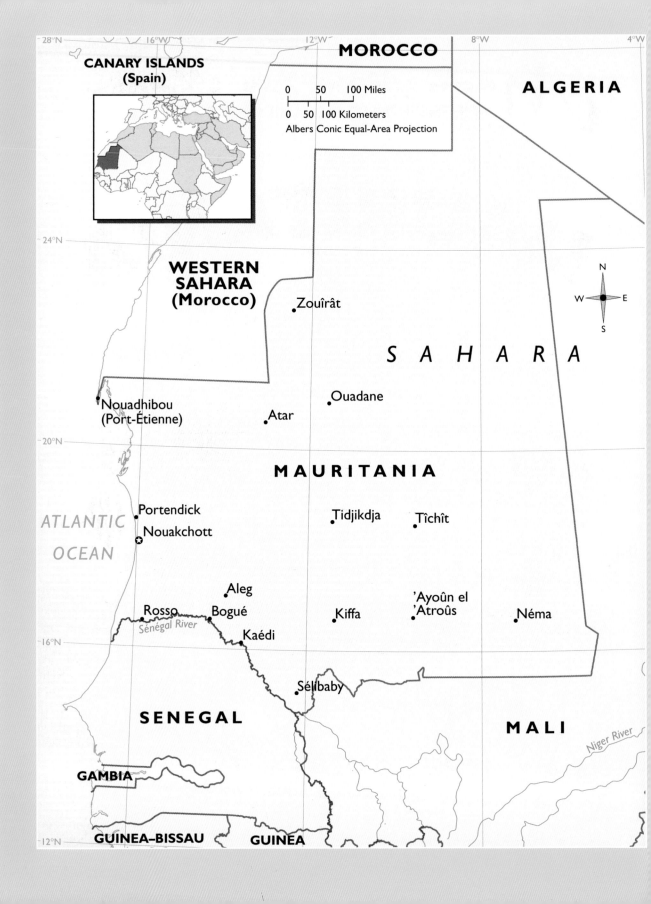

Modern Middle East Nations
AND THEIR STRATEGIC PLACE IN THE WORLD

MAURITANIA

JAMES MORROW

MASON CREST PUBLISHERS
PHILADELPHIA

Produced by OTTN Publishing, Stockton, New Jersey

Mason Crest Publishers
370 Reed Road
Broomall, PA 19008
www.masoncrest.com

3 5 7 9 8 6 4 2

Library of Congress Cataloging-in-Publication Data

Morrow, James, 1974-
  Mauritania / James Morrow.
     p. cm. -- (Modern Middle East nations and their strategic place in the world)
  Summary: Discusses the geography, history, economy, government,
  religion, people, foreign relations, and major cities of Mauritania.
  Includes bibliographical references and index.
   ISBN 1-59084-526-9
  1. Mauritania--Juvenile literature. [1. Mauritania.] I. Title. II. Series.
  DT554.22.M67 2003
  966.1--dc21

                                                                    2003004138

TABLE OF CONTENTS

Modern Middle East Nations
AND THEIR STRATEGIC PLACE IN THE WORLD

ALGERIA
BAHRAIN
DJIBOUTI
EGYPT
IRAN
IRAQ
ISRAEL
JORDAN
KUWAIT
LEBANON
LIBYA
MAURITANIA
MOROCCO
OMAN
THE PALESTINIANS
QATAR
SAUDI ARABIA
SOMALIA
SUDAN
SYRIA
TUNISIA
TURKEY
UNITED ARAB EMIRATES
YEMEN
THE MIDDLE EAST: FACTS AND FIGURES

Dr. Harvey Sicherman, president and director of the Foreign Policy Research Institute, is the author of such books as *America the Vulnerable: Our Military Problems and How to Fix Them* (2002) and *Palestinian Autonomy, Self-Government and Peace* (1993).

Introduction

by Dr. Harvey Sicherman

Situated as it is between Africa, Europe, and the Far East, the Middle East has played a unique role in world history. Often described as the birthplace of religions (notably Judaism, Christianity, and Islam) and the cradle of civilizations (Egypt, Mesopotamia, Persia), this region and its peoples have given humanity some of its most precious possessions. At the same time, the Middle East has had more than its share of conflicts. The area is strewn with the ruins of fortifications and the cemeteries of combatants, not to speak of modern arsenals for war.

Today, more than ever, Americans are aware that events in the Middle East can affect our security and prosperity. The United States has a considerable military, political, and economic presence throughout much of the region. Developments there regularly find their way onto the front pages of our newspapers and the screens of our television sets.

Still, it is fair to say that most Middle Eastern countries remain a mystery, their cultures and religions barely known, their peoples and politics confusing and strange. The purpose of this book series is to change that, to educate the reader in the basic facts about the 23 states and many peoples that make up the region. (For our purpose, the Middle East also includes the North African states linked by ethnicity, language, and religion to the Arabs, as well as Somalia and Mauritania, which are African but share the Muslim religion and are members of the Arab League.) A notable feature of the series is the integration of geography, demography, and history; economics and politics; culture and religion. The careful student will learn much that he or she needs to know about ever so important lands.

A few general observations are in order as an introduction to the subject matter.

The first has to do with history and politics. The modern Middle East is full of ancient sites and peoples who trace their lineage and literature to antiquity. Many commentators also attribute the Middle East's political conflicts to grievances and rivalries from the distant past. While history is often invoked, the truth is that the modern Middle East political system dates only from the 1920s and was largely created by the British and the French, the victors of World War I. Such states as Algeria, Iraq, Israel, Jordan, Kuwait, Saudi Arabia, Syria, Turkey, and the United Arab Emirates did not exist before 1914—they became independent between 1920 and 1971. Others, such as Egypt and Iran, were dominated by outside powers until well after World War II. Before 1914, most of the region's states were either controlled by the Turkish-run Ottoman Empire or owed allegiance to the Ottoman sultan. (The sultan was also the caliph or highest religious authority in Islam, in the line of the prophet Muhammad's successors, according to the beliefs of the majority of Muslims known as the Sunni.) It was this imperial Muslim system that was ended by the largely British military victory over the Ottomans in World War I. Few of the leaders who emerged in the wake of this event were happy with the territories they were assigned or the borders, which were often drawn by Europeans. Yet, the system has endured despite many efforts to change it.

The second observation has to do with economics, demography, and natural resources. The Middle Eastern peoples live in a region of often dramatic geographical contrasts: vast parched deserts and high mountains, some with year-round snow; stone-hard volcanic rifts and lush semi-tropical valleys; extremely dry and extremely wet conditions, sometimes separated by only a few miles; large permanent rivers and wadis, riverbeds dry as a bone until winter rains send torrents of flood from the mountains to the sea. In ancient times, a very skilled agriculture made the Middle East the breadbasket of the Roman Empire, and its trade carried luxury fabrics, foods, and spices both East and West.

Most recently, however, the Middle East has become more known for a single commodity—oil, which is unevenly distributed and largely concentrated in the Persian Gulf and Arabian Peninsula (although large pockets are also to be found in Algeria, Libya, and other sites). There are also new, potentially lucrative offshore gas fields in the Eastern Mediterranean.

This uneven distribution of wealth has been compounded by demographics. Birth rates are very high, but the countries with the most oil are often lightly populated. Over the last decade, Middle East populations under the age of 20 have grown enormously. How will these young people be educated? Where will they work? The failure of most governments in the region to give their people skills and jobs (with notable exceptions such as Israel) has also contributed to large out-migrations. Many have gone to Europe; many others work in other Middle Eastern countries, supporting their families from afar.

Another unsettling situation is the heavy pressure both people and industry have put on vital resources. Chronic water shortages plague the region. Air quality, public sanitation, and health services in the big cities are also seriously overburdened. There are solutions to these problems, but they require a cooperative approach that is sorely lacking.

A third important observation is the role of religion in the Middle East. Americans, who take separation of church and state for granted, should know that most countries in the region either proclaim their countries to be Muslim or allow a very large role for that religion in public life. Among those with predominantly Muslim populations, Turkey alone describes itself as secular and prohibits avowedly religious parties in the political system. Lebanon was a Christian-dominated state, and Israel continues to be a Jewish state. While both strongly emphasize secular politics, religion plays an enormous role in culture, daily life, and legislation. It is also important to recall that Islamic law (*Sharia*) permits people to practice Judaism and Christianity in Muslim states but only as *Dhimmi*, protected but very second-class citizens.

Fourth, the American student of the modern Middle East will be impressed by the varieties of one-man, centralized rule, very unlike the workings of Western democracies. There are monarchies, some with traditional methods of consultation for tribal elders and even ordinary citizens, in Saudi Arabia and many Gulf States; kings with limited but still important parliaments (such as in Jordan and

Morocco); and military and civilian dictatorships, some (such as Syria) even operating on the hereditary principle (Hafez al Assad's son Bashar succeeded him). Turkey is a practicing democracy, although a special role is given to the military that limits what any government can do. Israel operates the freest democracy, albeit constricted by emergency regulations (such as military censorship) due to the Arab-Israeli conflict.

In conclusion, the MODERN MIDDLE EAST NATIONS series will engage imagination and interest simply because it covers an area of such great importance to the United States. Americans may be relative latecomers to the affairs of this region, but our involvement there will endure. We at the Foreign Policy Research Institute hope that these books will kindle a lifelong interest in the fascinating and significant Middle East.

A lone camel surveys the broad sands of the Sahara Desert. Mauritania, which lies on the northwest coast of Africa, is a tiny country that is mostly covered with desert. Yet there is much that can be learned from this land and its history.

Place in the World

Because of its vast size and apparent emptiness, the Sahara Desert is one of those places that students and travelers are either immediately attracted to or repelled from. Some see the desert as a place of stark, empty beauty unpolluted by human contact or development. Others take the opposite view, look at the vast spaces between seemingly tiny settlements on the map, and say, "Why bother?"

But most casual observers, no matter what their opinion is on the desert, are usually misinformed. Although the Sahara Desert is vast and largely uninhabited, it is hardly a place devoid of settlement or history. For thousands of years humans have built their civilizations around this seemingly vast emptiness, and much of the cultures of these early settlers remains to this day. Careful study of the Sahara and the people who live there can be quite rewarding. It is a place where students can learn about such varied subjects as global environmental history, the rise of Islam, and the European colonial experience in Africa. And a country like Mauritania is a wonderful place to begin such studies.

Although at first glance Mauritania might look like a large, undeveloped area that time has forgotten, nothing could be further from the truth. While the Sahara Desert is what defines both Mauritania and the entire region of Africa in which it sits, this desert has been the scene of thousands of years of history, connecting empires, trading routes, tribes, and religions. Indeed, Mauritania's ancient history suggests that thousands of years ago, the country wasn't sandy desert, but a lush and fertile land that has only slowly dried out as the Sahara has spread south.

For students of the modern world, Mauritania has long been a fascinating laboratory of social history, and a place where the script of history has presented surprises. For example, until the middle of the 20th century Mauritania was a colony of France. This European power controlled other colonies in Africa and the rest of the world, and gained a reputation for brutality because of its exploits in Algeria, Mauritania's neighbor in North Africa. However, France's relationship with Mauritania was unlike its relationship with other African colonies. For much of the time that the French operated within Mauritania, they had to pay the locals for this privilege— something that is rarely seen in such colonial relationships. And because the French never interfered in any significant manner with Mauritania's local social customs and institutions, the country offers an unique window into ways of life that have gone largely unchanged for centuries.

This can be seen through Mauritania's experiences with the often-difficult subjects of race and religion. As in most places, these two controversial topics have created both positive and negative experiences for Mauritania, and it is worthwhile to study how the two issues have played out over the years. Almost the entire popu-

A man walks past a car covered with sand in the village of Boumdeid, near Kiffa. Desertification—the continuing spread of the Sahara Desert—has become a major problem in Mauritania during the past few decades.

lation of the country practices Islam, one of the world's great **monotheistic** religions. This is a faith that explicitly bans racial prejudice, teaching that all Muslims are the same in the eyes of Allah (God). However, racial divisions in the country, between the **Maure** populations of the north and the black African people of the south, remain a problem. The differences between these groups have contributed to accusations of unfairness in Mauritania's political system. These same differences have drawn the country into military conflict with its neighbors in the years since Mauritania became an independent nation.

Finally, in a world increasingly concerned with the state of the environment, Mauritania provides an important case study because its environment has, over thousands of years, evolved from moist and lush to dry and stark. The way the people of Mauritania have changed with these changes, and made them work for them,

A slave herdsman stands near goats near Chegar, Mauritania. The country is one of the few places in the world where slavery remains common, particularly of black Africans by the Maure population. Although the government officially outlawed slavery in the early 1980s, independent observers complain that it has never prosecuted people who hold slaves—or even admitted that slavery is still practiced. "The government of Mauritania refuses to follow through on its responsibility to abolish slavery not only in principle, but in practice," Adotei Akwei, a director of the international human-rights organization Amnesty International, said in 2002. "If it wishes to take its place amongst civilized, modern states, the Mauritanian government must put an end to this miserable assault on human dignity and freedom."

is an inspiring story of man's ability to adapt—and in some cases even thrive—in the harshest of conditions.

Mauritania is not a place that one studies because of its great role in history or human conflict; its role has been minor when compared to the larger dramas of other countries. Yet its history is important because the student of today can learn much from Mauritania. Whether the issue is the spread of deserts ("desertification"), the spread of Islam, or the spread of European colonialism, and later, African independence movements, Mauritania has its own unique stories to tell. And it is these stories—of Mauritania's people and culture—that make the country a unique and fascinating land to study.

Sand dunes at Chinguetti, on the western edge of the Sahara Desert. This land around Chinguetti was once fertile; however, changing weather patterns over the past 40 years have caused the desert to expand deeper into Mauritania.

The Land

Located at the western end of the Sahara Desert, Mauritania's land mass of nearly 400,000 square miles (a little more than a million square kilometers, or about three times the size of the state of New Mexico) is mostly dry and arid, and about 75 percent of the country is considered to be "desert" or "near-desert" in climate. The country is, however, not entirely barren; there is a substantial coastline of 469 miles (754 km), a hilly area in the center of the country, and grasslands and pasture in the south that support farming and ranching. In addition, Mauritania is rich in a few natural resources, particularly iron ore.

ONCE A LAND OF PLENTY

The world's weather is not a constant thing. It is always changing, and has been ever since the Earth formed. This has been especially true in the Sahara Desert, which has grown considerably over the past several thousand years and continues to spread even today. Some of the earliest evidence of this comes from paintings and engravings that archaeologists estimate to be at least six or seven thousand years old that have been found in Mauritania and its neighbors in the desert. These ancient carvings and paintings indicate that the Sahara region was once lush, fertile, and teeming with animal life—much like Africa south of the Sahara Desert is today. As one study of the Sahara colorfully puts it:

> Six or seven thousand years ago, in the early Neolithic times, a journey through the Sahara would have been very much like a safari in the game parks of sub-Saharan Africa today. Giraffe, ostrich, elephant, rhinoceros, buffalo, lion, leopard, warthog and many species of antelope and gazelle roamed the savannah [or flat grasslands] and wooded uplands (which, on evidence of fossilized pollen grains, supported wild olive, alder, lime, holm oak and cypress). Crocodiles and hippopotamuses swam in the many rivers and lagoons.

Interestingly, too, these paintings also suggest how the population of the area now known as the Sahara has changed. Today much of the region is populated by the descendants of lighter-skinned **Berbers** and Arabs (called Maures, or sometimes Moors). These are relative latecomers to the region—they arrived in waves between the third and twelfth centuries. However, the ancient Saharan paintings and carvings are very similar to those made by black Africans in the southern part of the continent. This fact suggests that blacks initially inhabited the area. They may have moved south to find more fertile lands, or been forced out by the arrival of the Berbers.

The notion of Mauritania as a lush land, and not a desert one, is borne out by many travelers who recorded their impressions of the place over time. In A.D. 22, the Roman writer Strabo described Mauritania as a fertile country, except for a small area which was desert, and said the region was supplied with water by rivers and lakes. He wrote:

> It has forests of trees of vast size, and the soil produces everything. It is this country which furnishes the Romans with tables formed of one piece of wood, of the largest dimensions, and most beautifully variegated. The rivers are said to contain crocodiles and other kinds of animals similar to those in the Nile. Some suppose that even the sources of the Nile are near the extremities of Mauritania. In a certain river leeches are bred seven cubits in length, with gills, pierced through with holes, through which they respire. This country is also said to produce a vine, the girth of which two men can scarcely compass, and bearing bunches of grapes of about a cubit in size. All plants and pot-herbs are tall, as the arum and dracontium [snake-weed]; the stalks of the staphylinus [thought to be parsnip], the hippomarathum [fennel], and the scolymus [artichoke] are twelve cubits in height and four palms in thickness. The country is the fruitful nurse of large serpents, elephants, antelopes, buffaloes, and similar animals; of lions also and panthers. It produces weasels equal in size and similar to cats, except that their noses are more prominent, and multitudes of apes, of which Poseidonius relates that when he was sailing from Gades to Italy, and approached the coast of Africa, he saw a forest low upon the sea-shore full of these animals, some on the trees, others on the ground, and some giving suck to their young. He was amused also with seeing some with large dugs [breasts], some bald, others with ruptures and exhibiting to view various effects of disease.

THE COMING OF THE DESERT

In the past millennium, however, changes in climate and farming practices have turned Mauritania into a country that is almost entirely sandy and infertile. Since the 1960s, changes in weather patterns, combined with the destruction

Changing weather patterns have caused the Sahara Desert to expand in Mauritania, as well as other countries in the region.

of forests and overgrazing of livestock, have caused the sandy desert to expand rapidly throughout the country. As the dunes take over, wells dry up and villages become engulfed in sand, thus making them uninhabitable. Even the capital city is no longer sitting on a fertile stretch of coastline. Today, most of Mauritania's agriculture is centered around a 250-mile-long (402 km) strip of land along the north side of the Senegal River, and it is here that most of the country's food is produced. Otherwise, in the words of one popular guidebook, in this very large country, "the biggest attraction . . . is the very desolation that keeps so many people away. For those with the true spirit of adventure, Mauritania is one of the least trodden spots in the world."

The Geography of Mauritania

Location: Northern Africa, bordering the North Atlantic Ocean, between Senegal and Western Sahara
Area: slightly larger than three times the size of New Mexico
    total: 397,953 square miles (1,030,700 sq km)
    land: 397,838 square miles (1,030,400 sq km)
    water: 116 square miles (300 sq km)
Borders: Algeria, 288 miles (463 km); Mali, 1,390 miles (2,237 km); Senegal, 505 miles (813 km); Western Sahara, 970 miles (1,561 km); coastline, 469 miles (754 km)
Climate: desert; constantly hot, dry, dusty
Terrain: mostly barren, flat plains of the Sahara; some central hills
Elevation extremes:
    lowest point: Sebkha de Ndrhamcha, 10 feet (3 meters) below sea level
    highest point: Kediet Tjill, 2,986 feet (910 meters)
Natural hazards: dust and sand-laden sirocco wind blows primarily in March and April; periodic droughts

Source: Adapted from CIA World Factbook, 2002.

As this map shows, much of Mauritania is low-lying sandy desert. There are very few parts of the country that rise as high as 1,640 feet (500 meters); the highest point in Mauritania, Kediet Tjill, is just 2,986 feet (910 meters).

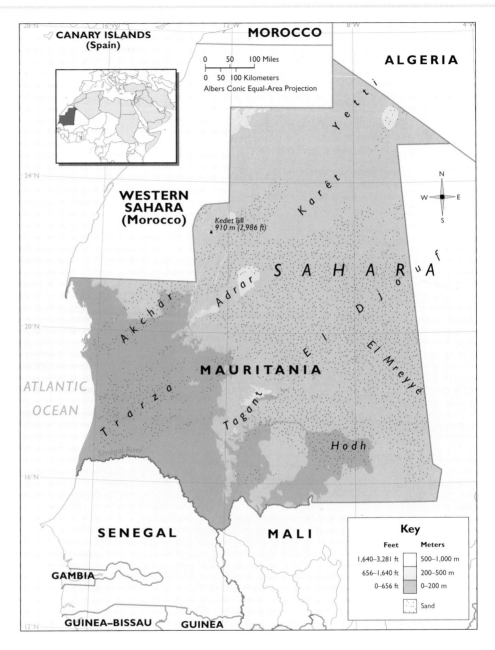

Away from the fertile strip in the south, most of Mauritania is stark, bleak desert. Even the capital city Nouakchott, which gives Mauritania a window on the rest of the world through its seaport, is largely covered in sand. When the modern city was founded in 1958, things were different, but a series of droughts pushed the desert to the city's doorstep. But to say that Mauritania is all sandy desert would be incorrect. Geologically, Mauritania boasts some of the most dramatic features in the entire Sahara Desert. In the country's western desert, dramatic low sandstone cliffs—formed by the breaking of a layer of rock millions of years ago—serve as important landmarks. They break the monotony of the thousands of square miles of barren desert around them, and

There is more vegetation in the southern part of Mauritania than in the northern area. Most of the country's farmland and pastureland is located along the Senegal River, which marks the country's southern boundary.

for centuries they have provided travelers with something to navigate by. Even today, people crossing the Mauritanian desert—whether by camel or in off-road, four-wheel-drive vehicles—use these cliffs to stay oriented and headed in the right direction.

Through much of the rest of the Mauritanian desert, however, the picture is bleaker and, for the traveler, more dangerous. Quicksand is a constant danger. So are deep valleys in which careless drivers can easily become stuck. And, of course, there is the ever-present danger of sandstorms and weather, which can be scorching hot during the day and surprisingly cold at night.

But perhaps the most scary and dramatic of Mauritania's features are not the high cliffs or low valleys, but rather the country's flat gravel plains, or **reg**, which stretch all the way from Algeria straight through the eastern part of Mauritania. These are, in the words of photojournalist Jeremy Swift, "the quintessential Saharan landscape." Of these plains, which stretch across several countries in the area, Swift also writes, "the Tanezrouft is a typical *reg*—four times the size of England and a major hazard for the . . . nomads who cross it in a series of forced marches with the sheep they take from the Adrar n Iforas to the markets in Algeria. There are only half a dozen wells and to miss one or find it dry is probably to die."

Moving west from these desolate plains, Mauritania's landscape becomes more diverse. In the northeastern part of the country, just inside the border with Morocco, are a series of dark mountain peaks making up the Kediet Tjill mountain range; their summits reach as high as 2,986 feet (910 meters). This is a very important region for Mauritania economically, because these mountains are rich in iron ore, which has been commercially mined for decades. (However, the difficulty involved with getting something as heavy and cumbersome as iron ore out of the ground and out of the desert presents unique and serious challenges for engineers).

This rock carving of a rhinoceros, found in the Western Sahara near Mauritania, is one of many signs indicating that at one time the climate of the region was much different from today.

WILDLIFE IN MAURITANIA

Despite the desolation of much of its land area, Mauritania manages to support some degree of wildlife. The country's southern flood plains support a wide variety of bird life—including a number of endangered species—especially when the Senegal River crests. Two other creatures thrive throughout the rest of the country: the camel and the ***addax***.

Most people know of the camel through popular culture. A popular image is of the so-called "ship of the desert" carrying an Arab or Bedouin tribesman and all his possessions through a lonely landscape. The camel was introduced to the region by Arab invaders who were spreading their new faith, Islam, to the region more than a thousand years ago. Today, camels are still used regularly to cross the desert.

In addition to the camel, Mauritania also supports one of the world's rarest, most endangered creatures—an animal that is also wonderfully suited to life in this harsh terrain. That animal is the addax, a type of antelope that, under normal conditions, never drinks a drop of water.

Addaxes were once widespread in the Sahara. Some people believe that the ancient Egyptians domesticated these animals—archaeologists have found stone tablets recording the private ownership of at least one herd. Addaxes stand four feet high at the shoulder and sport a grayish white coat and large, spiraling dark horns. Although they look almost cow-like when they stand still (their bodies give them a somewhat heavy appearance), they can, when threatened, take off at a fast gallop across even sandy terrain, thanks to their broad hooves. The addax survives mostly by eating perennial grass tufts and bushes that are scattered throughout the Sahara. The animals will travel many miles in search of food.

Unfortunately, increasing dryness in the Sahara region over the past thousand years, coupled with the effects of widespread hunting by humans, has made life very hard for the addaxes. Although they can run for short distances, they are by nature slow creatures who can be exhausted by hunters driving camels or dogs, and tribesmen in the area have long believed that various parts of the animal are useful as medicine. In his 14th-century writings, the Arab traveler Ibn Battuta described the healing powers of medicine made from addax horn, and even today people in the region maintain that parts of an addax stomach can be used to heal scorpion bites or protect against witchcraft.

By the end of the 19th century, the addax had vanished from most of Africa; in the 1920s a party of French soldiers wiped out one of the last known major herds. Since then, the creatures are

The addax was once plentiful throughout the Sahara. Today, however, the animals are among the most endangered species in the world. They can still be found in remote areas of the Mauritanian Sahara. The addax does not need to drink water; it can get enough moisture from dew and from the plants it eats.

very rarely seen even in the most remote corners of the Mauritanian Sahara. Today efforts are underway to preserve the addax. This is done largely through zoo programs, since the animals breed well in captivity. Keeping the species alive in the wild in a country like Mauritania is tough simply because the conditions are so harsh and the area where they can roam is so vast. However, neighboring countries like Morocco and Tunisia have bred addaxes in captivity, then successfully reintroduced them to the wild, so it is hoped that similar programs may succeed in Mauritania.

An ancient walled Berber city. Berbers arrived in the region of modern-day Mauritania more than 1,600 years ago; Arabs followed them into the region in the eighth and ninth centuries. These two groups intermarried, becoming known as the Maures (or Moors).

History

M auritania's history encompasses the rising of African empires, the spread of a religion brought by traders from the deserts of the Arabian Peninsula, the arrival of French colonists, and the country's independence. Through all these phases of history, the region has been something of an outpost of empire—for the kingdoms of Africa, for the Arabs who brought a new religion with their conquests, and for the French, who at times seemed as if they wanted to hold the country simply to prevent rivals from gaining it. Yet as a result of this "outsider" or "outpost" status, Mauritania has preserved to some extent a culture that has in many ways gone unchanged for hundreds of years. Unlike other French colonies, such as Mauritania's northern neighbor Algeria— where the Europeans set about a program of remaking society in the image of the "mother country"—even under

This ancient African fertility figure is a relic of the Kingdom of Ghana. Black Africans lived in the Mauritania region before the arrival of the Maures, and the Kingdom of Ghana was an early power in the region.

foreign rule Mauritanians were largely allowed to continue living in their old ways.

Little is known about the ancient history of the Mauritania area. Archaeologists know that people lived in the region, and that the climate was less harsh than it is today. Mauritania and the entire **Sahel** region of northwest Africa was fertile and covered by what is known as savanna, or flowing grassland. Tribes living in the area included the Bafour, who lived on the coast, and the Toucouleur, and Wolof, who established their settlements in river valleys. These ancient people hunted, fished, raised livestock herds, and cultivated fields.

Although powerful city-states like Carthage and Rome controlled large areas of North Africa at different times between about 800 B.C. and A.D. 400, the desert areas of Mauritania apparently never interested either of these important ancient powers. But when traders introduced camels to the region during the first few centuries A.D., the seeds for commercial and cultural exchange were planted.

Although the Sahara has been called "one of the world's greatest barriers to human movement," the ability of camels to haul great loads over long distances without a constant supply of water (unlike other beasts of burden, such as horses), plus the desire of merchants to expand their markets, made conquering the desert possible. The creation of long-distance trading routes through West Africa, including Mauritania, would lead to the eventual settlement of the region by outsiders.

Among the new arrivals were the Berbers, a nomadic people of North Africa who arrived in the Mauritania region during the third and fourth centuries A.D. These Berbers conquered the Bafour and other tribesmen living in the northern region and established their own communities.

THE KINGDOM OF GHANA AND THE SANHADJA CONFEDERATION

By the sixth century, the Africans living in southern Mauritania had established a powerful empire in the region. The rulers of this empire controlled a vast area of land that included parts of modern-day Mauritania, Mali, and Senegal.

The Kingdom of Ghana was unique in a number of respects, not least of which was that its society was ***matrilineal***. Unlike most other royal families around the world (for example, the British monarchy), matrilineal descent decrees that the heir to the throne comes from the mother's line of descent.

The Kingdom of Ghana was based at Koumbi Saleh, located on modern Mauritania's southern border with Mali. At the time Koumbi Saleh had an important position between the Sahara Desert to the north and more fertile lands to the south. It was also a convenient stopping-off point for trade between western Africa and the rich lands of Egypt and the Middle East. The Kingdom of Ghana became wealthy through trading and gold mining; the rulers also received ***tribute*** from conquered tribal chieftains. In recent decades archaeologists have discovered the remains of what was once the wealthy capital city, including indications of multi-story buildings made of stone (a labor-intensive process in the absence of motorized machines) and extensive cemeteries and memorials honoring the prominent dead of the community. At the height of the kingdom's power, according to the 11th-century Arab geographer al-Bakri, who visited Ghana in A.D. 1067 and 1068, the king of Ghana had under his command some 200,000 soldiers and 40,000 archers. Al-Bakri also mentions the army's horses, which means that the army of Ghana may have been among the first in western Africa to use mounted soldiers.

Al-Bakri also left descriptions of life in this ancient capital city. The king never communicated with his subjects directly. Instead, a hierarchy of government ministers carried out his orders. In addition, the king was considered almost divine, and was the object of worship for a special religious cult. The members of this sect consisted of an elite priesthood whose members would practice their religion outside the city in an area of secluded groves. When the king died, he would be buried—along with a large group of loyal assistants, as also happened in other African kingdoms like those of ancient Egypt—under a gigantic dome-like mound of timber and soil. Al-Bakri described the ritual:

> When the king dies, they build a huge dome of wood over the burial place. Then they bring him on a bed lightly covered, and put him inside the dome. At his side they place his ornaments, his arms and the vessels from which he used to eat and drink, filled with food and beverages. They bring in those men who used to serve his food and drink. Then they close the door of the dome and cover it with mats and other materials. People gather and pile earth over it until it becomes like a large mound. Then they dig a ditch around it so that it can be reached only from one place. They sacrifice to their dead and make offerings of intoxicating drinks.

Northern Mauritania, meanwhile, was taking shape under a less dramatic, but no less impressive, political group. The Sanhadja

Confederation was a loose affiliation of several Berber tribes, who took advantage of the introduction of the camel to form a powerful trading network in the northern part of the country. This political organization encompassed both the nomadic Berbers, with their traditional religion and way of life, and the Berber merchants who traveled along the trade routes.

The traders of the Sanhadja Confederation were not rivals to the Ghana empire. In fact, the Sanhadja Confederation seem to have been an important trading partner; the southern end of their trade routes was Koumbi Saleh, where Sanhadja traders found a great market for goods from other parts of the region. The Sanhadja Confederation was at the peak of its power from the eighth through the tenth centuries. After this its important communities were assimilated into the Kingdom of Ghana.

Despite the trade cooperation between the north and south, there was no union. Ultimately, it was religion, not trade, which would bring unity of a sort to the region.

THE RISE OF ISLAM

Like other nations of North Africa, the modern history of Mauritania has been greatly influenced by a man named Muhammad. His spiritual transformation on the Arabian Peninsula more than 1,400 years ago would eventually develop into one of the world's most important religions. A consequence of this would be the great cohesive force of Islamization in the region.

Muhammad was born in Mecca, a city on the Arabian Peninsula, around A.D. 570. At the time, the people of this region followed a variety of pagan and *polytheistic* religions. Muhammad was orphaned as a boy, so he grew up under the protection of an uncle who trained him as a merchant and trader. When Muhammad was in his twenties, he married a wealthy widow, Khadija, with whom he raised four daughters; two sons died as infants. And for some 15

This colored engraving shows Muhammad receiving his first vision in a cave on Mount Hira Jabal al-Nur, located near Mecca. Around the year 610 A.D. the angel Gabriel commanded Muhammad to spread the message that there was one god, Allah. Muhammad received many visions from Allah; these are recorded in the Qur'an (or Koran), the holy book of Islam.

years, he enjoyed a peaceful and prosperous life as a respected member of society.

Muhammad's focus changed, however, when he began to experience visions in the desert. According to legend, he was on a spiritual retreat in a mountain cave outside Mecca when the angel Gabriel appeared, instructing him:

> Recite in the name of thy Lord who created,
> Created man from a clot;
> Recite in the name of thy Lord,
> Who taught by the pen,
> Taught man what he knew not.

The Angel Gabriel told Muhammad that he was to be the prophet, or messenger, of Allah, the one true god. Muhammad then had other visions about the nature of Allah. Eventually, the angel told Muhammad to begin sharing his revelations with others. Muhammad began to teach the messages that had been revealed to him through his visions, and he soon attracted followers.

But over the next 12 years, as Muhammad continued to preach about the revelations he had received from Allah, the religious leaders of Mecca grew angry. They resented Muhammad's unceasing condemnation of the polytheism practiced by most people of Mecca, and plotted to kill him. When Muhammad learned of the plot, he fled to Medina, another city on the Arabian Peninsula. (At the time this city was known as Yathrib; it was located at an oasis 11 days away from Mecca by camel.)

Muhammad's journey to Medina in A.D. 622—known as the *hegira*—became a signal episode of the Islamic Era. Muhammad's preaching in Medina would drive his campaign to present Allah's revelations, to defeat those who denied that his revelations were divine messages, and to achieve temporal as well as spiritual sanctification. In Medina new religious traditions were established,

Hundreds of thousands of Muslims pray before the Kabba, which is located in the Great Mosque at Mecca. Like those who followed the polytheistic Arab religions that preceded Islam, Muslims consider the Kabba to be the center of the earth, and the most sacred place of worship. Kabba means "square" or "four sides," and the stone's sides are said to represent the four directions: north, east, south, and west.

such as praying in the direction of the **Kabba** stone in Mecca, an item originally held sacred by the non-Muslim tribes of Arabia. At this point the new faith, which would be known as Islam (from the Arabic word for "submission," specifically to the will of God), was born.

Muhammad died just 10 years later, in 632, after having dictated the **Qur'an** (or Koran), the holy book of Islam. His fledgling religion would very likely have died soon after, were it not for the commitment and devotion of his followers and the system of caliphs (the Arabic word *caliph* means "deputy of the prophet") devised to keep the faith going after the prophet's death. This system allowed for a continual, stable leadership to take charge of the religion and direct its **adherents**. Under the leadership of the caliphs the Arab Muslims made war on neighboring tribes. Soon,

This decorated page from the Qur'an dates from the 12th century. It was produced during Almohad rule over North Africa. Islam has been the dominant religion of the region since the 7th century.

they had extended their rule throughout the Arabian Peninsula, as well as into neighboring Persia (modern-day Iran). In the process, much of the population of the newly conquered areas converted to Islam, sometimes by agreement and sometimes through compulsion.

It wasn't long before Islam was to move beyond the Arabian Peninsula. Expansion into North Africa was logical because of its close proximity. By 641, Islam had made its way into Egypt, and as a result of expeditions that took place from 642 to 669, the religion had spread throughout North Africa and was starting to filter into Mauritania. By the early eighth century, Islam was dominant in the northwest of Africa, an area also referred to as the **Maghrib**. Many Berber tribesmen, including those in Mauritania, had converted to Islam and helped the invading Arabian tribes to spread the religion across the deserts of northwest Africa.

Despite their common religion, the Berbers and Arabs did not always coexist peacefully. The Berbers were historically resistant to outside control, and they did not want to be ruled by the recent Arab invaders. The Arabs didn't help matters much either, as they did not work to ensure peaceful relations with the Berber Muslims. Because the Berbers were converts to Islam, and had not been born into the faith, the Arabs felt that they could treat them at times as second-class citizens—despite the Islamic belief that all people are equal before God. This inequality between Arabs and Berbers took many forms. Berbers found themselves liable to pay heavy and burdensome taxes and were even made slaves in some cases (even though according to Islamic writings a Muslim could not enslave another Muslim). Ironically, in Mauritania, the descendants of these Berbers would later practice many of the same hated discriminations they complained about against the black Africans of the south.

The disputes culminated in a rebellion against the caliphate that lasted from 739–740. When it was all over, the rebels (who declared themselves "Kharijites," from an Arabic term meaning "those who secede") had broken up the uniform practice of the faith. Consequently, as a variety of ***theocratic*** kingdoms sprang up throughout the region, different practices emerged, not all of them strictly Islamic. In a number of these kingdoms, education and learning prevailed, and they became important centers of mathematics, astronomy, and law.

In Mauritania, meanwhile, Islam would hold sway for centuries. The country itself would be an outpost of the faith and remain a way station for traders and travelers.

ARAB INVASIONS AND THE FALL OF EMPIRE

By the time the Arab geographer al-Bakri arrived in the Kingdom of Ghana, Islam was already established in the kingdom.

Koumbi Saleh had grown into two cities: the ancient imperial one from which the kings of Ghana had ruled their holdings for five centuries, and a newer Muslim town, where adherents of the new faith lived and worked and prayed at one of several mosques recently built in the settlement. In the 11th century, a group of Berber Muslims, the **Almoravids** (this name literally means soldiers from the peripheral or frontier areas), invaded and conquered the whole of the West Saharan area. Their faith was a more structured and rigorous version of Islam and they pushed their interpretation of the religion on people in the region—sometimes violently. Until this point, Islam was practiced by some

An Almoravid shrine in North Africa. During the 11th and 12th centuries the Almoravids, a Berber dynasty, ruled an area that included present-day Mauritania, the Western Sahara territory, and the coastal areas of Morocco and Algeria, as well as the southern and eastern regions of Spain.

Berbers, mostly those living in cities who were more interested in trading and living their lives than spreading Islam. The Berbers who lived in the desert had continued to practice their own ancient religious traditions. The Almoravids, however, were involved in creating an orthodox Islam and putting an end to practices they saw as heretical.

Almoravid power began to grow when an Islamic leader, Abd Allah Ibn Yassin, and his followers settled into a monastic kind of living that began to attract many of the Sanhadja Berbers. In A.D. 1042, Ibn Yassin declared a jihad, or holy war, to oppose those of the Sanhadja who resisted his version of Islam. The goal of his followers was to create a community wholly devoted to Islam.

The Almoravids first conquered the Djodala, offering the Djodalans the choice of converting to Islam or being put to death. After this, the Almoravids began to draw to their side other Berber tribes of the western Sahara. In these conquests, the Almoravids had in essence recreated the Sanhadja Confederation; this time, however, the people were united through faith and religious goals.

The Almoravids would conquer Sijilmasa, the northern center of the caravan trade, in 1054, and then Aoudaghast, previously the capital of the Sanhadja Confederation, where an important mosque was located. Aoudaghast would remain a prominent city until the 16th century.

In 1059, the charismatic Ibn Yassin died; his successors were Abu Bakr ibn Unas in the south and Yusuf ibn Tashfin in the north. Ibn Tashfin was to prove a formidable leader. He and his followers took Morocco and made Marrakech their capital city in 1062. Their campaign continued its victories through 1082 until they had captured nearly the entire western Maghrib. Their success prompted the Andalusian Muslims of the Iberian Peninsula to seek their support in fighting the Christians, who were led by the Spanish King Alfonso. Ibn Tashfin and his soldiers rescued the Andalusians, demolished the armies of the Spanish Christians, and established Islamic law and Almoravid dominion over the south of Spain.

Abu Bakr ibn Unas, the other important Almoravid leader of this time period, attacked and overcame the powerful Kingdom of Ghana. This effort would take some 14 years—from 1062 through 1076—before the strongly fortified city of Koumbi Saleh was brought down. Though the kingdom was not finished by this defeat, its power was sorely diminished and the Almoravids maintained their dominance over the region. From Mauritania, Almoravid power spanned from Senegal to Spain.

After the deaths of Abu Bakr and Ibn Tashfin, interior conflict between the Sanhadja Berbers and a reformist group during the 12th century would bring about the end of the Almoravid Empire. However, the cohesive power the Almoravids and the Sanhadja had created in their Islamization of the Western Sahara had the greatest influence on the Mauritania region and its people.

Islamization's greatest growth would occur when Yemeni Arabs entered Mauritania in the 12th and 13th centuries. A vital part of this period was the rise of Sufism, a movement that grew out of opposition to Islam's increasing focus on religious law at the expense of human spiritual needs. Within Sunni Islam, Sufism was a renewing of the emphasis on faith as the route to union with Allah. Its practitioners, called Sufis, saw the Qur'an as a Muslim's guide to a spiritual union with God, while mysticism provided the route to the presence of God. The notion that intermediators could function as facilitators in the union of a believer and God led to the concept of brotherhoods and the ***marabouts***. They were to become the guides in establishing Islamic education. Marabout is a title of sorts often given to a brotherhood leader, but it has a larger meaning in that any religious leader may be called a marabout. He often is a teacher who forwards the faith through his ***probity*** and spirituality. A marabout may fulfill numerous roles, such as providing spiritual healing for the sick or negotiation for those who need intervention in affairs too difficult to resolve without help. Since the 13th century Sufism has continued to support the spiritual and emotional needs of Muslims.

THE COMING OF THE EUROPEANS

As Europe emerged from its Dark Ages, European rulers began to learn more about the world around them. They saw the great resources of Africa and Asia, and wished to establish and control trade routes that would help their countries to prosper. Among the first countries to send out voyages of exploration and discovery were the Portuguese. A member of Portugal's royal family named Prince

St. Louis Island as it appears today. The French first established a permanent settlement here in the early 19th century, and would eventually control a large part of western Africa.

Henry sponsored a number of expeditions along the coast of Africa in the 15th century. Henry's goal was to see if ships could sail around Africa and reach Asia and the Spice Islands (modern-day Indonesia). He believed there was great wealth to be found in Africa, and he also wanted to establish contact with a legendary Christian kingdom believed to be located somewhere on the continent. As the Portuguese explored the western coast of Africa, they established trading posts in Mauritania and other areas. They found that slaves could be easily captured or acquired on the African coast, and soon the Portuguese were shipping thousands of African slaves each year.

In the 16th century, other European powers followed the lead of Portugal—Spain, the Netherlands, and France. The Dutch became great traders of gum arabic, which is used in the printing of patterns on textiles. The Mauritanian variety of gum arabic was believed to be far superior to that grown in any other locale. Late in the 17th century, the French would oust the Dutch from Mauritania and establish a permanent outpost on the coast at Saint Louis. Eventually the British would force the French from the West African coast; France would not return until the 1815 Congress of Vienna recognized French claims on African territory. All of these countries were interested in trading along the coast, and attempted to negotiate advantageous treaties with the Maures who were dominant in the region.

The Maures were not entirely victims of these recent arrivals from Europe. Instead they learned to manipulate the newcomers by setting one European exploiter against another, and by requiring a payoff from all. With the arrival of the French in the area, this annual payment came to be known as the *coutume*.

In the early part of the 19th century, however, Muhammad al Habib, **amir** of Trarza, became an active opponent of the French. He tried to extended his domain through marriage to the heiress of the Oualo Kingdom, which was located in modern-day Senegal—a region

Louis Faidherbe (1818–1889) served with the French army as it attempted to assert control over the interior of Algeria during the 1840s. As colonial governor of the Senegal-Mauritania area, Faidherbe strengthened French rule in the area by conquering the Maures. Faidherbe later served with French forces during the Franco-Prussian War.

France considered part of its sphere of influence. When Habib began to market gum arabic directly to England, France's rival, the French perceived this as a hostile act. In 1825 they retaliated by sending troops to attack the amir's forces. After this victory, France decided that in order to control the region, they would have to build fortifications along the Senegal River. This was a key waterway because it is the only permanent river in northwestern Africa that flows to the Atlantic Ocean. By 1840, the French had built fortified settlements along the northern bank of the Senegal River, in present-day Mauritania. From this stronghold France intended to control all the nearby African lands.

In 1854, Louis Faidherbe became the French governor of the area. Louis Napoleon, the ruler of France, ordered Faidherbe to end the *coutume* and strengthen the French settlements to protect both colonists and the gum arabic trade. To accomplish this, Faidherbe conquered the Oualo Kingdom, as well as the cities of Trarza and Brakna, ultimately defeating the forces of the Maures in 1856. In the treaties ending the war, the French negotiated an end to the *coutume*; in its place, the French agreed to pay the Maures 3 percent of the total value of gum arabic exported each year. This would help increase the gum arabic trade and keep the peace: it was in the Maures best interests not to disrupt French shipments of the resource.

French control of the area remained strong while Faidherbe was governor (1854–61 and 1863–65), but after he left office his successors allowed power to slip away. By the late 1870s, the Maures had continued resisting French control, attacking villages and forcing the administrators to resume the *coutume*. Fighting between Maure tribes was also common. French companies often supplied the weapons with which the Maures fought each other and the French government.

At the beginning of the 20th century, France established a simple plan for its African colonies: divide and rule. Xavier Coppolani, a Corsican brought up in Algeria, created the policy, which became known as "peaceful penetration." Coppolani would eventually be known in France as the father of the colony of Mauritania; to the locals, he was known as the "Pacific Conqueror."

Coppolani's idea was simple. He wanted to enlist the support of three key marabouts who held great power in the Senegal-Mauritania area by offering what has been called the "Pax Gallica" or "French Peace." This "Pax Gallica" would come when the French, with their administrative system and military strength, arrived and became closely involved in the region. This would stop the activities of warring clans and tribes that were making life miserable and dangerous in Mauritania.

By 1904 Coppolani had gotten two of the three marabouts to sign on to his plan, which he pushed past administrators in Senegal (who were not interested in acquiring what they saw as desert wasteland to the north) and French arms makers who continued to profit from the tribal warfare. He was able to "pacify" much of central and southern Mauritania, taking several key towns and outposts in the process and arranging for French troops to be stationed there. Only the third marabout, Shaykh Ma al Aynin, who held sway in the north, resisted the plan. And since he was in control of northern Mauritania—specifically the strategically important town of Adrar—he was able to play France against local rival Morocco for power. Thus when Coppolani was killed in 1905, Aynin was able to extend his reach, rallying Maures with promises of help from Morocco and calls for a jihad to drive the French back across the Senegal River.

But Aynin's moment of glory was not to last. A French colonel named Henri Gouraud, who was seasoned in defeating resistance in the colonies, assumed control of the French armies in 1908. He soon captured Atar, a key city in the Adrar region. A French victory was complete by 1912, with Adrar and southern Mauritania in submission. Thus the French reputation as fierce fighters was firmly fixed and the dominance of the French-supported marabouts from the south over the warriors was accomplished.

THE BIRTH OF MAURITANIA

Until Coppolani came along, Mauritania was not considered very important by the French government. Their concerns focused on controlling their far-flung empire, and they saw Mauritania as useless desert that was part of Senegal. But in 1904, thanks to Coppolani, France would acknowledge Mauritania as distinct from Senegal and as valuable in its own right as a French-protected territory. Thus Mauritania became a civil territory to be governed by a chief government administrator.

For the next 16 years, Mauritania was considered separate from French West Africa (Afrique Occidentale Française, or AOF), a collection of French territories in the region. In 1920, Mauritania was linked politically with seven other territories that made up French West Africa—Senegal, French Sudan (now called Mali), French Guinea (now called Guinea), Ivory Coast (now called Cote d'Ivoire), Dahomey (now called Benin), Niger, and Upper Volta (now

A modern-day marabout praying in North Africa. The term *marabout* is of French origin, and is used to refer to a particularly devout Muslim, often a hermit. In the early 20th century, the marabouts of Mauritania had a great deal of authority among the people, and the French tried to convince the religious leaders to go along with French plans to pacify the colony.

called Burkina Faso). It would remain part of French West Africa until 1946.

Mauritania was run in a similar fashion to other French colonies in the region, but there were some very important differences. Unlike France's other possessions in West Africa, most of the administrative regions were still subject to military leaders. Administrators came in and out, and the boundaries of Mauritania were frequently altered. These confusing circumstances arose because the military powers rarely agreed with the civilian leaders and vice versa. But more important was the role that traditional Maure chiefs were to play in the administration. Unlike other West African territories of France, to some degree the native leaders of Mauritania ruled their people.

(In many ways, French policy in Mauritania, while an exception to their general rule for running things abroad, was taken from the British model of empire, which was very much concerned with using local chieftains to help control territory.)

In order to keep peace in Mauritania, the French appointed tribal leaders who would function as rulers while part of the French administration. Among the chieftains who were appointed were the amirs of Trarza, Brakna, and Adrar. To assist these three, the French added 50 rulers of more minor tribes and some 800 chiefs of very small groups. Although the French selected the tribal leaders, their selections had to be approved by an administrative council from each tribe.

Also, the French government in Mauritania depended on the marabouts to assist in ruling the land and maintaining control. They rewarded the marabouts richly for cooperating. For example,

Charles de Gaulle (1890–1970) was a French general during World War II; after the fall of France to Nazi Germany in June 1940 he escaped to lead the Free French government from exile. Many people in Mauritania joined the French resistance, which attempted to sabotage the Nazi occupation. North Africa was liberated by the Allies in 1942, France was freed from Nazi occupation in 1944, and Germany was defeated in May 1945. More than a decade later, protests in Algeria helped bring de Gaulle to power as president of France. His government allowed many of the French colonies in Africa, including Mauritania, to become independent.

to express gratitude for one marabout's support the French gave him control of a highly regarded school for Islamic studies. The French so trusted the marabouts, who traditionally meted out justice in accordance with Islamic law, that they allowed them to continue implementing the traditional laws without overseeing them or enforcing the laws of France.

In other words, although France had authority over Mauritania, within the country the tribal leaders and marabouts continued to wield great power. This pushed the Mauritanians into a more modern social configuration while allowing them to maintain their own societal structure. This is in stark contrast to the French experience in other African colonies. For example, in Algeria the French government undertook an intensive program that attempted to remake all of Algerian society to conform to the image of French society. This plan ultimately failed, and led to the bloody Algerian war for independence (1954–1962).

When World War II began in 1939, men and supplies from Africa were appropriated for the French war effort. But France fell quickly to Nazi Germany in June 1940. Some of the French leaders fled from the country and set up a government in exile; they became known as the Free French, and they continued fighting against Germany. In France after the surrender, however, a new administration, based in the city of Vichy, was established; it collaborated extensively with the Nazis. With the Vichy government of France in control of the country's African holdings, Nazi-inspired policies of racial discrimination were instituted. Democratic ordinances concerning work and land ownership in Mauritania were thrown out. Instead, the people were forced to work harder to supply food for the Nazis.

After the war ended, a constitution was proposed that would link the colonies together with France, giving all residents equal status and the right to vote. In addition, Mauritania and each of the other colonies would receive a greater degree of administrative freedom. Independence, however, was not an option for the African colonies at this time. The French remained firmly committed to pursuing the idea of assimilation that would play out so tragically in Algeria and elsewhere.

As an impoverished and underdeveloped territory, in Mauritania there was little in the way of political consciousness or a desire for independence either before or immediately after the Second World War. Until 1946 Mauritania was part of French West Africa, which had only one representative in the French Senate. The French constitution created in that year established Mauritania as an entity separate from French West Africa and entitled to its own representation in the French National Assembly. However, universal suffrage was still not a reality—only a small percentage of the people of Mauritania were allowed to participate in the election for France's assembly that year.

The Mauritanian Entente, their country's first political party, was created for the 1946 election, and Horma Ould Babana became the party's first deputy in the French National Assembly. Babana had been elected on a platform advocating independence from France. However, he was ineffective during his five year term; worse, he was in Paris most of the time and out of touch with opinions and politics at home in Mauritania. In the 1951 election Babana lost to the candidate of another party, the Mauritanian Progressive Union (MPU), which was supported by the marabouts and the French colonial administration. In a 1952 election for Mauritania's assembly, the MPU captured 22 of 24 seats.

Once in power, the MPU began making reforms. In 1956, the integrationist phase of French colonial policy was ended. Instead, France's overseas territories were given greater control over their own affairs. Universal voting rights and the creation of district and local representative councils meant greater freedom for the territories to determine their future. France still had the final say on such issues as relations with other countries, and continued to oversee Mauritania's educational system, supply its armed forces, and provide economic support. However, much of the power in France's West African colonies now rested with local leaders, rather than with the French government.

The 1956 reforms brought into existence a governmental body to take on high-level operations that had previously been the function of a colonial overseer assigned by the French. Taking the form of a committee or council, several Mauritanians, elected by their territorial parties and guided by the most prominent of their constituents,

Moktar Ould Daddah and Georges Pompidou, president of France from 1969 to 1974, wave to the crowd during a parade in Mauritania. Daddah, the first president of an independent Mauritania, served from 1960 to 1978.

were each in charge of a governmental operation. The vice president of the council was the appointed head of the ministers. Moktar Ould Daddah, a lawyer (the only one in Mauritania) descended from a clerical family who supported the French, was the first prime minister. He would soon become the first leader of an independent Mauritania.

INDEPENDENCE

The new self-government, although still under ultimate French authority, took office in May 1957. Nouakchott was chosen as the capital because of its location between two competitive groups—the Maures, based in Adrar, and the black farmers of the Senegal River Valley. This choice reflected Moktar Ould Daddah's political strategy: to change the country's destructive competition between Maures and blacks into unity through compromise.

Daddah's goal—to achieve conciliation and unity among the diverse population—was a formidable undertaking. The country could be divided into northern and southern regions. In the south were black Africans who lived as peasant farmers, while the north was populated by desert nomads of Arab or Berber descent—the Arabic-speaking Maures, who thought of themselves as belonging to an Arab-Islamic populace. From the mingling of blacks and Maures, a third group had evolved. These people were racially either black, or mixed Maure and black, and shared the cultural traits of the Maures. Many were held by the Maures as slaves.

Prime Minister Daddah's regime faced the threat of secession by both the Maures from northern Mauritania, who threatened to join with Morocco, and from the southern blacks, who could head to the Mali Federation. In both cases, the people would be joining countries that shared their ethnic backgrounds. Some high-profile Maures, like Horma Ould Babana and other leaders of the Mauritanian Entente, had already abandoned their country for

Morocco. Babana and the National Council of Mauritania Resistance supported the idea of Morocco annexing Mauritania. This was something the government of Morocco had proposed, believing that Morocco had a historical claim to the territory of northern Mauritania. In the south, black dissidents joined in the Gorgol Democratic Bloc, which was opposed to a merger with Morocco and wanted to preserve close relations with neighboring black African countries. In 1957, some of these dissidents formed the Union of the Inhabitants of the River Valley to defend their rights and oppose Maure control.

Another stumbling block in the Mauritanian path to independence was the continued French presence in the country. Those who wished to see Mauritania free of French control were cautious about anyone with ties to France. For example, Daddah had lived much of his life in France. When he returned to Mauritania, groups like the Association of Mauritanian Youth, an organization that strongly supported complete independence from France, initially opposed Daddah's policies.

Daddah's amiable relationship with the French would serve Mauritania well during this time, however. With the French authorities strongly behind him, he calmed the rising tide of secession and brought stability to the political situation, putting unity at the forefront. The Mauritanian Regroupment Party came into existence at the 1958 Congress of Aleg. It was made up of members of the Mauritanian Progressive Union, the Gorgol Democratic Bloc, and those members of the Mauritanian Entente who did not follow Babana's leadership. Daddah was chosen as secretary-general, or head of the party, with Sidi el Moktar appointed president. In 1959 the Mauritanian Regroupment Party declared that it opposed incorporation by Morocco, and also did not agree with a French plan to unite Mauritania with several other French territories in the Common Saharan States Organization. Instead, the party's leaders

Native dancers celebrate Mauritania's independence, December 1, 1960.

wished for Mauritania to become a member of the French Community. This was intended to be an organization of former French colonies around the world, which would become autonomous states but would remain loosely tied to France.

At the same time, however, events outside of Mauritania were contributing to the country's movement toward complete independence. In France's most important North African colony, Algeria, a nationalist uprising had begun in 1954; rioting and violence in Algiers early in 1958 led to the collapse of France's government, which was known as the Fourth Republic. General Charles de Gaulle, a French hero of World War II, was called from retirement to oversee the creation of a new French government in June 1958. A new national constitution was adopted in September, and by December 1958 de Gaulle had been elected president.

The governmental turmoil in France and the independence movement in Algeria inspired other French colonies in Africa to seek complete independence outside of the French Community. In March 1959, Mauritania adopted a constitution in place of the French constitution, and the country's leaders began to prepare for independence.

Although Mauritania was close to becoming an independent state, ethnic and regional diversity continued to interfere with the consolidation necessary to create governmental strength. By his focus on the goal of independence, Daddah succeeded in gaining support from diverse groups. He did this in part by ignoring past differences and oppositions of these groups. He also took a conciliatory approach, and attempted to incorporate his detractors, as well as his supporters, into the government. Daddah also promised to include blacks, as well as Maures, in the national government. As a result, even those who disagreed with Daddah's policies worked with him to achieve the common goal. The rise of a group of young and progressive opposition leaders, who formed the Mauritanian National

Renaissance Party (Nahda), illustrates this. When members of Nahda were accused of corruption, Daddah prohibited them from participating in the first elections to Mauritania's National Assembly. Daddah was strict in his punishment of Nahda, even jailing a number of the group's leaders. Yet because he treated the group fairly and openly, Nahda respected Daddah. It obeyed his request to support the fledgling National Assembly's accomplishments. When the next election under the new constitution occurred, Nahda worked for Daddah's election, as did the Mauritanian National Union, which represented the black constituency. On November 28, 1960, Mauritania declared its independence from France.

In September of 1961, when the first elected government of the new nation convened, among those holding important ministerial positions were candidates who had represented the Mauritanian National Renaissance Party as well as those who had stood for the Mauritanian National Union. The new coalition, to be called PPM (Parti du Peuple Mauritanienne), was formed by the union of the Mauritanian Regroupment Party, the Mauritanian National Union, the Mauritanian Muslim Socialist Union, and Nahda. It became the single Mauritanian governmental entity. Among its new governmental policies was the provision that no alignment or connections with France would exist.

Daddah supported his policy of inclusion by giving cabinet posts to two blacks, thus fulfilling the government's goal of gaining black advocacy. Moreover, a black would head the National Assembly, which included 10 ten black members and 20 Maures. Daddah himself continued to accumulate power to further strengthen the single party. In 1964 the PPM coalition government declared Mauritania a one-party state, and in 1965 the constitution was amended to pronounce PPM the only legitimate party in Mauritania. Whatever opposition might arise would be contained and handled in prescibed paths of communication within the PPM.

The Daddah regime remained in power until 1978. By then several years of conflict with Morocco over the Western Sahara territory (known as the Desert War) had become so costly and so divisive that Daddah's government was overthrown. In July 1978, Colonel Mustapha Ould Salek, one of Daddah's military commanders, supplanted him as the head of government.

TURMOIL AND INSTABILITY

Mauritania was about to undergo a difficult period of turmoil. Salek, despite his promises to the contrary, was unable to do anything about the conflict in the Western Sahara, which had resulted from a dispute between Morocco and the Algerian-backed Polisario movement that was fighting for the territory's independence. In addition, he faced dissension in the southern part of the country because of a smear campaign, put forth by Senegal, to create the impression that the Maure leader was racially insensitive to his black constituents. Salek did little to help matters when most of the people he appointed to his national advisory committee were Maures.

Within a year Salek's government was overthrown. On April 6, 1979, Colonel Ahmed Ould Bouceif and Colonel Mohamed Khouna Haidalla formed the Military Committee for National Salvation (CMSN) to take control of the country. Just a month later, Ahmed Bouceif was killed in a plane crash, and Mohamed Haidalla took control of Mauritania.

Haidalla's first task was to disengage from the Western Sahara conflict. This he did in the summer of 1979, agreeing to hand over Mauritania's portion of the Western Sahara—about one-third of the territory—to the Polisario. However, Haidalla made no attempt to prevent Morocco, which claimed two-thirds of the Western Sahara, from preempting the Polisario and extending control over the entire territory—which Morocco did in 1981. Mauritania, Haidalla

Mauritanian President Maaouya Ould Taya (left) speaks with Abdoulaye Wade, president of Senegal. Taya seized power in 1984, and has maintained control over the country through force and rigged elections.

proclaimed, was neutral on the question of the Western Sahara.

Among Haidalla's other accomplishments were formally abolishing slavery in the early 1980s (the French had made attempts to do this, but had been unsuccessful). This made him popular with the country's southern blacks. However, although the government ruled that slavery was officially illegal, independent observers found that the practice persisted in Mauritania.

Despite these accomplishments, Haidalla's opponents both in and out of Mauritania (including former leader Moktar Ould Daddah), were working to unseat him. In January of 1983 a Libya-supported coup to oust Haidalla failed. By the next year, however, many Mauritanians were disenchanted with what they saw as corruption and mismanagement in Haidalla's government. In December 1984 Colonel Maaouya Ould Sid'Ahmed Taya took advantage of Haidalla's absence on an overseas trip to seize power. Taya has ruled ever since, maintaining control by barring opposition parties and presenting the façade of democracy by holding periodic elections, which are widely regarded by independent observers as corrupt.

Controversies over Taya's legitimacy as ruler of Mauritania not withstanding, the country has made a great deal of progress both domestically and internationally under the current regime. But it has not been without its challenges. In what are now known as "the events of 1989," Taya faced his greatest challenge: a border war with Senegal that would eventually lead to Mauritania forcibly deporting tens of thousands of its own citizens across the river. What started as a dispute between two farmers over land rights quickly escalated into brutal ethnic conflict on both sides of the river—across which artillery fire was exchanged at one point—and 40,000 Mauritanians were forced to flee their homeland. This, along with other revelations about human rights' abuses in Mauritania and Taya's tilt toward Saddam Hussein during the 1991 Gulf War, led to what many in the West regard as the low point of any modern Mauritanian government.

Yet Taya has also surprised many observers. In recent years he has presided over something of a modernization of Mauritanian society, increasing education and the rights of women while fending off the appeal of Islamic fundamentalism that has caused problems in other Muslim countries, including nearby Algeria, which was embroiled in a civil war over this issue during the 1990s and early 2000s. And although he supported Iraq's 1990 invasion and annexation of Kuwait (an ironic stance for the leader of a country that had long worried about being gobbled up by Morocco), since then Taya has led his country to establish full diplomatic relations with Israel—making it one of only three Arab nations to do so—and to substantially strengthen Mauritania's ties to the West.

A mosque in Nouakchott. Islam is the official religion in Mauritania, and practically all of the country's people are Muslims. The practice of other religions is discouraged by the government.

Politics, Religion, and the Economy

Mauritania's government may call itself a democracy, but most observers believe this is not the case. According to the U.S. State Department's 2001 report on human rights in Mauritania, the country's most recent elections are widely regarded as having been fraudulent, because the government in Nouakchott dissolved the only major opposition party in 2000. The State Department also pointedly adds that "democratic institutions remain rudimentary, and the government circumscribes citizens' ability to change their government."

The president of Mauritania, Maaouya Ould Sid'Ahmed Taya, came to power in a military coup in 1984 and has been at the forefront of Mauritanian political life ever since—first as head of a military government, then as chief of state of the civilian government as head of the Social Democratic

Republican Party (SDRP). But even though Mauritania has shifted in recent years from a military dictatorship to an ostensible democracy, Taya's government in Nouakchott still holds most political control. Mauritania is divided into 13 administrative regions (including one that contains the capital territory, Nouakchott), and in the past few years the country has moved slowly toward decentralizing power.

Along with the executive branch in Nouakchott, Mauritania also has a **bicameral** legislature. In other words, the legislature includes two "houses," just as the United States has an upper house (the Senate) and a lower house (the House of Representatives). Mauritanian elections for legislators are held every two years for members of the Senate and every five years for the National Assembly. Mauritanians receive the right to vote at age 18; unlike other Islamic countries of North Africa, women are permitted to vote for their representatives. Women are also allowed to stand as candidates for government positions, although relatively few have been elected to the legislature.

Although Taya disbanded the main opposition party in the year 2000, multiple political parties do exist in Mauritania—although most of these are based more on the concept of tribal loyalty than they are on shared political goals. The U.S. State Department notes, "Politics in Mauritania have always been heavily influenced by personalities, with any leader's ability to exercise political power dependent upon control over resources; perceived ability or integrity; and tribal, ethnic, family, and personal considerations. Conflict between white Moor, black Moor, and non-Moor ethnic groups, centering on language, land tenure, and other issues, continues to be the dominant challenge to national unity."

Still, in news that encouraged many observers, in 2002 and 2003 Taya's government held talks with the main opposition party, the Opposition Progress Party. In announcing the meetings,

The crescent, star, and color green depicted on the flag of Mauritania are all traditional symbols of Islam.

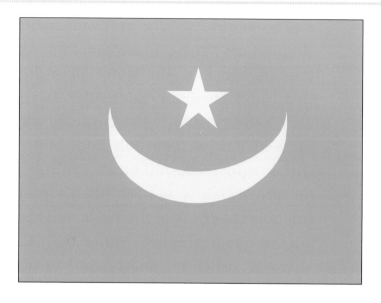

representatives from the SDRP said that they were taking a cue from other African states, which have liberalized their regimes in recent years.

Along with the president and the legislature, Mauritania also has a supreme court, a court of appeals, and a series of lower courts, all of which enforce a legal code that is a combination of Islamic law and French civil law, a holdover from colonial times.

A LAND OF ONE FAITH

Mauritania is an entirely Muslim nation—there is virtually no one in the entire country who does not accept the Qur'an as the holy book. But what does it mean to be a Muslim? And, more specifically, what does it mean to be a Muslim in Mauritania? The answer is not as straightforward as one might think.

Islam grew out of the Arabian Peninsula 1,500 years ago, and today about a billion people adhere to the faith. Along with Christianity and Judaism, it is one of the three great monotheistic religions. As such, there are some similarities in doctrine and belief between Islam and these other religions, but there are also important differences.

The central prayer and statement of belief for Muslims is a simple one: "There is no god but Allah, and Muhammad is his prophet." In fact, the word *Allah* literally translates as "the one God," and Muslims claim Allah is the same God worshipped by Jews and Christians. Muslims also accept the Old Testament scriptures as part of their holy literature, though they believe that the Qur'an supersedes all other writings. They regard Muhammad as the greatest and last of Allah's prophets. Muslims include the teachings of Jesus in their religion, though they believe that he was another great prophet, rather than the son of God. Muslims also share a belief in angels with Christians and Jews; in fact, Muhammad's original religious vision is believed to have been of the Angel Gabriel. Moreover, like Christians, Muslims look forward to a final "day of judgment" on which the world as we know it will end and the wicked and the just will go to their ultimate rewards.

But this is where the similarities end. Along with these general foundations of belief that tie Islam to the other, older faiths, Muslims also subscribe to what they call the "five pillars."

First is belief in Allah and his prophet Muhammad. The statement of belief is called the *shahadah*, and it is required of all followers of Islam: "I believe that there is no god but Allah, and Muhammad is his prophet."

The second pillar of Islam is prayer (*salat*). Five times a day at specified times, devout Muslims are expected to stop what they are doing, bow down in the direction of Mecca, and say their devotions.

The third of Islam's precepts is charity (*zakat*). To Muslims, charity is one of the highest virtues, whether it involves giving to a poor beggar or helping a traveler who needs a place to stay for the night. And while the doctrine that all Muslims should give a fixed proportion of their income to the poor is considered to purify the soul of the giver, it also has a practical benefit. With everyone required to give money to the poor, the practice, at least in theory, eliminates the need for state-sponsored social welfare in Islamic societies.

Fasting (*sawm*) is the fourth pillar of Islam. Muslims are required to fast regularly, a practice considered to be purifying. During Ramadan, the ninth month of the Islamic calendar (which is based on the cycles of the moon), Muslims are supposed to avoid eating, drinking, and certain other activities from sunup to sundown. Going without water and food all day can be difficult, especially in the harsh climate of Mauritania and other desert areas where the faith is practiced. A solution for many of the faithful in Mauritania is to stay inside all day, then break the fast after night falls by eating with their families.

Pilgrimage (*hajj*) is the fifth pillar of Islam. Every male Muslim is

The Economy of Mauritania

Gross domestic product (GDP*): $1.03 billion
GDP per capita: $350
Inflation: 4.4%
Natural resources: iron ore, gypsum, copper, phosphate, diamonds, gold, oil, fish.
Agriculture (25% of GDP): dates, millet, sorghum, rice, corn, dates, cattle, sheep
Industry (29% of GDP): fish processing, mining of iron ore and gypsum
Services (46% of GDP): government, shipping, other
Foreign trade:
    Imports—$335 million: machinery and equipment, petroleum products, capital goods, foodstuffs, consumer goods (2000)
    Exports—$359 million: iron ore, fish and fish products, gold (2000)
Currency exchange rate: 261.75 Ouguiyas = U.S. $1 (January 2003)

*GDP, or gross domestic product, is the total value of goods and services produced in a country annually.
All figures are for 2001 unless otherwise indicated.
Sources: World Bank; CIA World Factbook, 2002.

required to make a pilgrimage to the holy cities of Mecca and Medina once in his life, if he can afford it. Women, too, can make the pilgrimage, but it is not required of them. Every year millions of Muslims make the journey at an appointed time to pray at a series of holy sites in an impressive display of humility and devotion. It is considered quite special for a Muslim to make the pilgrimage, and those who have accomplished it often wear white skullcaps and take the honorific title "Hajji."

Islam affects many aspects of daily life for Mauritanians. Because of the nature of the religion, which does not make any distinction between the rules of governments and the rule of God, Mauritania and most other majority-Muslim states use Islamic law (**Sharia**) as a guide for making rules and regulations to govern the people.

In some Islamic countries, such as Saudi Arabia or Sudan, *Sharia* laws are imposed harshly and without appeal. The individual behavior of every person in these countries is governed by *Sharia*, whether or not they are Muslim. Everything from how a woman dresses to what a person can eat and drink is governed by this code.

The laws of modern Mauritania are a combination of secular (that is, non-religious) laws and *Sharia*. According to the Mauritanian constitution, Islam is the country's official religion, and in theory that is the faith of every Mauritanian. However, the government has reportedly been tolerant toward the few Christian citizens in its ranks (a statistically insignificant number, less than 1 percent) and to non-Muslim foreigners working in the country. Unlike in some other Muslim countries such as Saudi Arabia, no attempt is made to restrict the private worship of non-Muslims. However, non-Muslims are not permitted to attempt to convert Mauritanians to their faith. Proselytizing is viewed as an effort to undermine Mauritanian society. As a result, organizations such as Christian-aid groups must limit their activities to providing humanitarian or technical assistance.

One aspect of life in Islamic states that is always controversial concerns the treatment of women. In this regard, Mauritania is more progressive than many other Muslim states, but it has a long way to go before catching up with the more liberal Western world. In legal proceedings, for example, the testimony of two women is required to equal the testimony of one man, according to the country's interpretation of *Sharia.* Also, a woman needs parental permission for her first marriage, although subsequent marriages do not require permission.

Still, there are signs that Mauritania has begun to recognize the contributions women make to the country's economy. Unlike other Muslim countries, for example, Mauritania has taken great strides to bring women into jobs that were traditionally taken by men— especially positions in the government or in the state-owned mining corporation. Mauritanian laws have been passed to ensure that women are paid the same as men if they do the same work. In addition, women have recently begun to be involved in the fishing industry, forming several women-owned fishing cooperatives and even advancing in the state's police force. In 2000, for example, Mauritania appointed the first female police commissioner and chief inspector in Nouakchott.

THE MAURITANIAN ECONOMY: AID, AGRICULTURE, AND IRON

Mauritania's economy relies on two main activities: agriculture (including fishing) and extractive industries, which involve the pulling of valuable commodities out of the ground for sale on world markets. It has, in the past several years, also relied on foreign aid at the rate of approximately $300 million per year as a consequence of the country's economic mismanagement, which has caused a series of budget shortfalls. However, a program of ***privatization***— that is, selling off government-owned industries to more efficient private companies—and a joint program with the World Bank have helped get Mauritania back on the road to economic growth and, it is hoped, to paying off its $2.1 billion national debt.

Agriculture is concentrated mostly in Mauritania's southern plains, just north of the Senegal River. Indeed, 47 percent of the country's population relies on farming for their livelihood. Among the agricultural products Mauritania grows—both for export and domestic consumption—are dates, millet, sorghum, rice, and corn, as well as beef and lamb. Mauritania is also blessed with a coastline that affords ready access to some of the best fishing grounds in the world, and fishing and fish processing remain a major industry. Unfortunately, overfishing both by Mauritanians and by fishing fleets from foreign countries threatens this valuable resource. Furthermore, a series of bad harvests dating back to 1996 have threatened much of Mauritanian agriculture for the time being, with many international aid organizations worried that the country could face famine—especially in the south.

But while agriculture and fishing have largely served to feed the

Two views of the fish market at Plage de Peche, Nouakchott. (Left) A woman sells fish from the beach. (Bottom) A Maure family sits in front of traditional fishing boats. Mauritania is near some of the best fishing waters in the world.

Mauritanian population, it is the extractive industries that have long been the country's key to accessing foreign markets and obtaining all-important foreign trade. More than a thousand years ago the Kingdom of Ghana relied on gold as a major source of wealth and as a means to trade with neighboring states. Today, though gold is still mined, iron ore has become the major commodity that has kept Mauritania afloat financially during the 20th century.

The existence of iron ore deposits in Mauritania has been acknowledged since at least the eleventh century, when the mountains just south and east of what is today Western Sahara were named Djbel le-Hadid (literally, "the iron mountains") by the Arabs. Today, these mountains—which are now known as the Kediet Tjill range—are a great source of both iron and quartz. And although the French discovered the existence of the iron ore deposits in 1934, it was not until 1951 that they decided to do something about it. In that year a group of French, British, and Canadian investors, engineers, and other interested parties recommended researching the possibilities of mining at F'derik, a relatively short distance inland from the Western Sahara. The next year, in 1952, the Societe des Mines de Fer de Mauritanie (or MIFERMA, the Iron Mining Society of Mauritania) was founded with investment by French, British, Italian, German, and Mauritanian parties. Over the next five years, a great deal of time and money was spent in solving the incredible problem of establishing in these remote desert mountains a mine from which the ore could be extracted, then transported to shipping points. This goal would require the construction of not only a mine, but also of towns where workers would live and of railways and airstrips to move men and material in and out. Construction did not begin until 1960.

Between April 1960 and June 1963, when the first shipments of iron ore rolled out to the port at Nouadhibou, the entire industrial infrastructure had to be established in the middle of the desert. Some

408 miles (650 km) of railway track and 32 miles (52 km) of roadway were constructed, a new port was dug, mines were established, and two new towns—each with a population of 5,000 people—were built, with all the services they required, including schools, hospitals, movie theaters and a supermarket. It was truly a Herculean effort. Perhaps the greatest obstacle was sand, across which it is incredibly hard to lay railroad tracks. Any person who has ever visited a beach will remember how their feet sink in the sand with every step, and will understand how difficult it is to keep hundreds of tons of locomotive and railway cars moving across sandy desert. Two trains, each more than a mile (2 km) long and pulled by four locomotives equipped with special air filters to keep sand out of the works, make the trip to the coast every day, and when one goes off the track, it is sometimes faster and easier to build a new track around the accident than to try to clear the mess immediately.

Largely because of these mining activities, Mauritania has been able to maintain a positive balance of trade—meaning that the country exports goods and services worth more than what it has to import, or buy from other countries. In 2001, for example, iron ore was Mauritania's number one export, and the country exported $359 million worth of products and imported $335 million worth. Perhaps the greatest problem Mauritania has, then, is integrating the wealth and modernity brought by the iron industry with the rest of the country: only 14 percent of Mauritanians are employed in the industrial sector, yet they are responsible for far more of the country's economic production than agriculture. Another problem is that the value of iron ore rises and falls with the economy. When iron's value declines, it causes economic hardships for Mauritania.

OIL: FUTURE RICHES FOR MAURITANIA?

Although iron has given Mauritania something of an advantage in world markets over the past few decades, the price of the

Iron ore is Mauritania's most important export, and Nouadhibou is one of the main ports from which this commodity is shipped. The ore is mined near Zouîrât and F'derik.

commodity was so depressed in the early years of the 21st century that iron was much less profitable to extract and sell. Fortunately, although Mauritania has never been thought of as an oil-rich state, recent advances in technology suggest that the country could have a future exporting petroleum products.

Oil exploration has been taking place off the coast of Mauritania since 2001. In September 2002, the government announced that several test wells drilled off the coast could "potentially [deliver] commercial hydrocarbons." The early expectations were that Mauritania might control as much as 110 million barrels of oil.

Because of unrest in the Middle East, particularly among oil-rich states such as Iraq, Saudi Arabia, and Kuwait, as Mauritania's oil industry develops the country will almost certainly find opportunities to sell its petroleum products to Western nations like the United States, which want to decrease their dependence on oil coming from the Persian Gulf.

A group of Maures in the capital of Mauritania, Nouakchott. The population of the country can be divided into three basic subgroups—white Maures, black Maures, and black Africans. Much of the power is held by the white Maures, who have historically subjugated members of the other groups.

The People

M auritanians are not a homogeneous people. Despite the fact that nearly all Mauritanians worship Allah, the god of Islam, the people of this country are divided by region, by ethnicity, and by tribal loyalties. A traveler moving from one end of Mauritania to the other would quickly realize that the people living in the north are from a different cultural universe than the people of the south, and that the daily life of a resident of a coastal city such as Nouakchott is completely foreign to a Mauritanian eking out a living in the desert or coastal plains. As a result, there is no single answer to what it means to be a Mauritanian.

To begin to understand Mauritanian life, one can start by taking a look at the numbers. Mauritania, with a land mass approximately three times that of the state of New Mexico, is home to more than 2.8 million people, according to 2002 estimates. (In contrast, New Mexico—itself a sparsely populated desert region—is home to about 1.8 million individuals.) And the Mauritanian population is growing at a rate of almost 3 percent per year, which is currently too much for the country's primitive and beleaguered health care system to cope with. Mauritania suffers from a very high infant mortality rate of more than 7.5 percent (by contrast, the infant mortality rate in the United States is less than .007 percent), and life expectancy for the average Mauritanian male is just 49 years, for women, just over 53 years (life expectancy is 74.5 years for men and 80.2 years for women in the United States).

These statistics only tell part of the story. The rest is that Mauritania is a multicultural nation, with at least three separate and distinct groups vying for power and recognition. Of the country's 2.8 million people, approximately 30 percent are what are known as "white Maures," another 40 percent are considered "black Maures," and the remaining 30 percent belong to various black tribes of sub-Saharan Africa. This last group includes members of several important African tribes—the Toucouleur, Wolof, Fulb, and Soninke. Much stake is put in tribal membership, and officials in the Mauritanian government are often chosen—and act—more on the basis of their loyalty to one group or another than as members of a diverse nation. These ethnic differences have posed some of Mauritania's greatest post-independence challenges.

(Opposite) As this map indicates, Mauritania is lightly populated. The country's population density is less than 8 people per square mile (3 people per square kilometer). Most of the people live around cities, or in the fertile strip along the Senegal River.

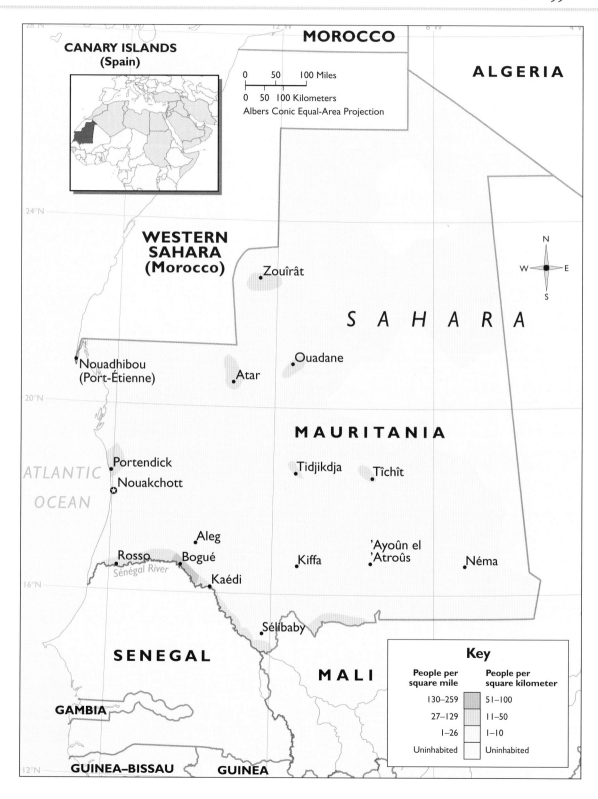

CANARY ISLANDS
(Spain)

MOROCCO

ALGERIA

0   50   100 Miles
0   50   100 Kilometers
Albers Conic Equal-Area Projection

WESTERN
SAHARA
(Morocco)

Zouîrât

S A H A R A

Nouadhibou
(Port-Étienne)

Ouadane

Atar

20°N

24°N

MAURITANIA

Portendick

Tidjikdja

Tîchît

Nouakchott

ATLANTIC

OCEAN

Aleg

Rosso   Bogué

'Ayoûn el
'Atroûs

Néma

Sénégal River

Kiffa

Kaédi

16°N

Sélibaby

SENEGAL

MALI

Key		
People per square mile	**People per square kilometer**	
130–259	51–100	
27–129	11–50	
1–26	1–10	
Uninhabited	Uninhabited	

GAMBIA

12°N

GUINEA–BISSAU   **GUINEA**

THE MAURES AND BLACK MAURITANIANS

Within Maure society, a complex class system exists that may initially be difficult for outsiders to figure out. A rigid hierarchy governs Maures, who consider non-Maures (black Africans) to be outsiders who simply should not figure into the equation of power in Mauritania. At the very top of Maure society are the warrior class, or *hassani*, and the class of religious leaders, or marabouts. The term *marabout* connotes someone who is not only a learned teacher of Islamic scripture, but also a person on whom Allah has conferred divine grace. As a consequence, marabouts are considered more able than others to mediate disputes.

Lower down the Maure class system are various artisans, craftsmen, and entertainers. (Entertainers, especially poets and musicians, are held in particularly high regard, though they are sometimes feared because of their supposed knowledge of the occult). These groups truly do form separate and distinct classes in Maure (and by extension, Mauritanian)

The People of Mauritania

Population: 2,828,858
Ethnic groups: mixed Maure/black 40%, Maure 30%, black 30%
Religions: Islam, 100%
Language: Hassaniya Arabic (official), Pulaar, Soninke, Wolof (official), French
Age structure:
    0–14 years: 46.1%
    15–64 years: 51.7%
    65 years and over: 2.2%
Population growth rate: 2.92%
Birth rate: 42.54 births/1,000 population
Death rate: 13.34 deaths/1,000 population
Infant mortality rate: 75.25 deaths/ 1,000 live births
Life expectancy at birth:
    total population: 51.53 years
    males: 49.42 years
    females: 53.71 years
Total fertility rate: 6.15 children born/woman
Literacy (age 15 and older): 41.2%

All figures are 2002 estimates.
Source: CIA World Factbook, 2002

society. There is little movement between classes; the children of craftsmen tend to marry only the children of other craftsmen, for example. There are few opportunities for movement out of a particular group.

At the bottom of the Maure class structure are the black Maures. As the name implies, members of this class are individuals whose ancestors intermarried with the local black African population. In the past black Maures have constituted something of a servant class in Mauritania. Indeed, in many cases, their ancestors were originally brought into Maure society as slaves. Although slavery was outlawed in Mauritania when the French arrived during the 19th century, it has nonetheless persisted. In the 1980s the government in Nouakchott passed laws

Signs in Mauritania are written in both Arabic, the official language, and French. A variety of African languages are spoken, and English can also be heard, particularly in the capital city.

Some Mauritanian children are educated in a medressa, or Islamic school. This is particularly true of Maure children living in rural parts of the country.

officially banning slavery. However, according to a 2002 report by the human-rights organization Amnesty International, "the government has not prosecuted a single offender for retaining a slave, or for buying or selling someone into slavery."

Outside of Maure society are the black Africans. Mostly concentrated in the southern section of the country, members of the various African tribes live, like the Maures, in highly stratified class systems with little room for movement. A noble class sits at the top of society in all African tribes in Mauritania, with a large segment of artisans, craftsmen, and merchants making up the middle classes. And a servile caste—often descended from slaves—sits at the bottom.

FAMILY LIFE IN MAURITANIA: CITY AND VILLAGE

The difference between city and rural life in Mauritania could not be more dramatic. Even if the capital city Nouakchott is not impressive because of size or comparative luxury, within the city lives an urbanized middle class who live, if not in great luxury, then at a level that comes close to that of their counterparts in Europe.

In villages, towns, and especially among the nomadic people of the desert, however, life is very different. In these places, adults and children alike tend to the basic business of survival—fetching water, tending the goats (which are used mainly for their milk; goats represent a large share of a family's assets, and are only killed for their meat on special occasions like Islamic festivals or weddings), and making trips to market towns to buy supplies. Here education is far more limited; often children spend a few years in a local Islamic **medressa**, learning about the Qur'an and how to read and write Arabic, but little more. They must leave school to help their families. Living in such a poor society and such a difficult environment requires all members of a family to work. There can be little wonder that although 86 percent of Mauritanian children now attend a school of some sort, just 41 percent of the adult population can read or write.

Yet family life among both Maures and black Africans is highly structured and valued. No matter the class in society, men sit at the top of the family, a place reserved for them both by tradition and the Qur'an. Islam permits men to marry up to four wives, and this is still practiced today—though in the cities, a growing professional class of women is making great strides, taking advantage of the Mauritanian government's attempts

Many Mauritanians admire but also fear poets, believing that they have access to and knowledge of the occult.

to modernize. And even in the rural areas women—especially white Maures—hold more power than their formal social status might suggest, regularly shuttling from village to town to city, trading, buying, and selling, contributing both to their families' livelihood and the overall economy.

EDUCATION

In examining Mauritanian education, one must look at two separate and distinct school systems: the Islamic schools, or medressas, and the secular schools that exist today as a legacy of French occupation. Islamic education has a long history—a thousand years or so—in Mauritania, and still represents a powerful, if decentralized, force in the country's cultural life. At these Islamic schools, students enter at approximately age eight (they will have already had a certain amount of schooling at home) and usually stay for seven years if they are boys and two years if they are girls. But while they will learn to read and write Arabic at these schools, students will learn little else besides that and the Qur'an from their marabout teachers. Still, a demand exists for this sort of schooling. In what today is Nouakchott, an institution of Islamic higher learning, the Institute of Islamic Studies, was founded in 1955. This school continues to attract students, drawing both from the city and from the countryside.

Secular education, a legacy of the French, is also required by the government for at least six years. And the Mauritanian government seems to take the responsibility of educating future generations seriously enough to spend more per pupil on schooling than most of its neighbors. Today, about 86 percent of school-age children attend school (child labor siphons off an unfortunately large portion of the population) and around a thousand students a year graduate from the University of Nouakchott.

One major controversy regarding Mauritanian education was the

A sampling of Berber textiles. Carpets and woven goods made in Mauritania and other parts of North Africa often have intricate patterns.

attempt to move the system away from the use of traditional French methods and language and towards the use of local languages such as Arabic. Attempts to "Arabicize" Mauritanian culture have met with fierce resistance from French-speaking black Mauritanians. In the 1970s a similar program was attempted in the schools that met with such resistance that it was eventually scrapped. Yet in the next decade, Mauritanian education made remarkable leaps as the government, responding to a shortage of skilled workers, encouraged the development of private and Islamic schools to increase literacy and the growth of facilities to teach children vocational skills. This was moved forward fairly rapidly because of a special loan from the World Bank in 1987 specifically earmarked to help Mauritania meet its educational needs. As a result the percentage of Mauritania's population able to read and write increased from less than 30 percent to more than 41 percent. By contrast, the literacy rate of countries like neighboring Mali and Senegal both hover around one-third of the population. However, the Mauritanian educational system still has a long way to go.

ARTS AND CULTURE

Poetry has long been considered an important art form in Mauritania—even if poets are sometimes regarded with a mixture of awe and suspicion for their power with words. But poetry is not the only form of cultural expression in Mauritania. Music is also important. A native type of folk music is popular; musicians play lutes and harps, accompanying vocalists to produce remarkable melodies. The songs tell the stories of the Mauritanians, their struggles and their victories. The singers of this poetic history are called griots, and the tradition extends centuries back into the past of West Africa. Their songs are the epics, stories that kept the history and culture of the region alive until it could be written down.

In terms of visual arts, the twin forces of Islam and necessity have long been the guiding forces in the creation of Mauritanian art. Traditionally, because of prohibitions in the Qur'an, Muslims avoid making "graven images" of living things; these are considered an affront to Allah. While more fundamentalist Islamic regimes have used this prohibition as an excuse to destroy the art of other cultures they encounter, in Mauritania, where a generally more tolerant incarnation of the faith is practiced, the traditional rule has led to the fantastically creative use of geometric patterns in areas such as carpet-weaving and jewelry-making.

Carpet-making, traditionally performed by women and more recently organized into village cooperatives, has been an especially important form of art in Mauritania. Carpets have been a part of Mauritanian culture since the first Arabs arrived a thousand years ago. Before they were prized around the world as works of decorative art, they were everyday objects used for a variety of purposes. Perhaps most famously, carpets have been used as prayer rugs. In mosques, although there is no religious requirement for their presence, carpets make worshippers (who must take off their shoes before entering the building) more comfortable, keeping their feet and knees from becoming cold as they bow and pray. And Muslim travelers have long carried so-called "prayer rugs" (traditionally, small rugs with a pattern that points to one end) to place on the ground facing in the direction of the holy city of Mecca while they recite their five daily prayers.

A Mauritanian Arab with his animals at the livestock market in Nouadhibou. This coastal town is the second-largest in Mauritania, with a population of 113,000.

Communities

When Mauritania and Senegal were separated in 1957, Mauritania was without a capital city. In response, the new government planned and built Nouakchott between 1958 and 1960 with an eye toward housing 200,000 residents. Since its construction, though, what may be the world's newest capital city has also become one of its most overcrowded, its population having swelled to more than 600,000 in the past four decades. As a result, the downtown area is surrounded by slums and shanty towns, which often consist of little more than gatherings of tents and shacks that lack connections to the electrical grid or sewage systems.

When the city was built, Nouakchott was in the middle of a fertile plain. However, this has changed with the rapid expansion of the Sahara Desert over the past several decades. Today the city is surrounded—and on many days, covered—by sand. Indeed, sand piles up against buildings in great drifts in the same way that snow accumulates in colder countries after a blizzard.

Despite its population, much of which is involved either in work for government agencies or in importing or exporting goods, Nouakchott is hardly a bustling metropolis. In fact, it's more of a large town, with goats and cars competing for space on the city's roadways, suggesting the early days when Nouakchott was just a small village and not an African capital. Among the more popular destinations for visitors and locals alike are the city's Atlantic coast beaches and the Port du Peche (literally, "fishing port"), where one can watch fishermen go about their business and perhaps enjoy a tasty seafood meal. The city has a National Museum, devoted to nomad life in Mauritania, and the National Carpet Office, where one can see handwoven rugs being made for sale and export. Although the French left Mauritania before Nouakchott became anything approaching the city it is today, they left a strong influence in the still-to-be-found excellent Paris-quality baked goods and coffee.

NOUADHIBOU

Also on the coast, but with a much longer history, Nouadhibou is a fishing town just a stone's throw (literally) from the Moroccan-

A variety of colorful wares are for sale in the bazaar in Atar, one of the older settlements in Mauritania.

controlled Western Sahara. Because of this proximity, this town of 113,000 people is often where people traveling in western Africa first enter Mauritania. From the rocky peninsula on which Nouadhibou sits, there is easy access to some of the most incredible marine life in the world, as well as a port for ships carrying iron ore abroad.

While Nouadhibou looks like a mere shipping and fishing town, the city has played an important role in Mauritania's modern history. In 1970 it was the location of a summit meeting at which the presidents of Mauritania and Algeria and the king of Morocco discussed the fate of the Western Sahara.

ATAR

Further inland from Nouadhibou is the old city of Atar, with a population of about 16,000 people. Based around an oasis, Atar has been an ancient meeting place for nomads in the region. Unfortunately, heavy flooding in 1990 damaged or destroyed much of the town's historic architecture, but there is still an old city with narrow streets and centuries-old structures. There is also a fort in the city that was built by the French during World War II. Besides its being founded on an oasis—which is today an impressively irrigated complex called the date palmerie—Atar is of practical significance as an important market town, serving a vast region of people who come in to buy and sell supplies, goods, and services.

ROSSO

In southern Mauritania along the border with Senegal is the town of Rosso. Its growing population, currently 63,000 people, is relatively large by Mauritanian standards, and it qualifies as a regional capital. Still, there is little of historical or academic signifi-cance, except that it serves as a busy trading post for its neighbors to the south in Senegal. The area around Rosso is also important because it sits amidst the fertile plains where most of Mauritania's agriculture grows. This has recently been aided by a $6 million joint venture between American and French concerns to increase farm production in the region.

CELEBRATIONS

Mauritania is, in the words of one guidebook, "not the best destination if you're looking for flamboyant, joyous displays of culture." Although the country's independence is celebrated on November 28, the most important celebrations in the Mauritanian calendar focus on the Islamic holidays. Because the Muslim calendar is based on the cycles of the moon and not the Western 365-day calendar, the dates of these events change from year to year. The most significant religious observances for Muslims everywhere—not just in Mauritania—are Ramadan, Eid al-Fitr, and Eid al-Adha.

Ramadan is a lunar month (meaning it lasts 28 days, or one moon cycle) during which Muslims are supposed to fast from sunrise to sunset, entirely leaving off eating, drinking (not even water), and smoking during those hours of the day, in the belief that one's spirit will be purified as a result of denying the body material and worldly pleasure. And, along with denying themselves food and drink, Muslims must practice spirituality, for all the good one does in a day's fasting can be undone by speaking poorly of another person, lying, or behaving in a jealous or covetous manner.

Many religions have annual forms of ritual fasting and self-denial, such as Yom Kippur in Judaism or Lent in Roman Catholicism. Ramadan is one of the most extreme such periods of any major faith. People in Mauritania, as they do in most Muslim countries, take the fast seriously, and streets are typically much less crowded during this period as people stay inside to keep cool and work, rest, or contemplate the Qur'an until night falls. When they are free to enjoy once more what they have denied themselves during the daylight hours.

If Ramadan is an occasion for self-denial, Eid al-Fitr is an occasion for celebration. This is perhaps the most important festival in the Islamic and Mauritanian calendar, as it marks the conclusion of Ramadan. Lasting three days, this is a great celebration as families get together in a spirit that could almost be compared to that of Christmas in the West. It is considered obligatory for Muslims to give a gift to the poor during this time, and children are traditionally also given presents and new clothes around this time. This is perhaps the most joyous time in the Muslim, and Mauritanian, calendar.

Another major festival of the Islamic calendar, the Eid al-Adha literally translates as "Festival of the Sacrifice." It commemorates the willingness of the patriarch Abraham to sacrifice his son to Allah. Muslim families in many countries, including Mauritania, will prepare a feast of goat or sheep to commemorate this event. Traditionally, the ritual of slaughtering the animal was done by the family who would eat it, but with more and more Mauritanians living in cities, this has become too difficult. The festival goes on for four days and takes place approximately three months after Eid al-Fitr. Eid al-Adha also marks the last day of the Islamic pilgrimage season, during which millions of Muslims travel to the holy cities of Mecca and Medina to fulfill their once-in-a-lifetime religious duty.

A U.S. warship fires a salvo in support of coalition forces fighting the Iraqi armies, which had invaded Kuwait in August 1990. Mauritania's support of Saddam Hussein during the Gulf War strained the country's ties with the United States, as well as with the Arab countries of the Gulf region.

Foreign Relations

auritania has had a complicated, and at times paradoxical, relationship with the United States, other Western democracies, and with Israel. Although the country is an Islamic state and a member of the Arab League, Mauritania is also one of just three Arab nations to have full diplomatic relations with Israel. Yet, the government in Nouakchott has also taken strong anti-Israel and anti-Western positions. It has urged citizens to demonstrate on behalf of the Palestinians during their *intifada* against Israel, and sided with Saddam Hussein during the 1991 Gulf War.

Mauritania has also had a rocky history with its African neighbors. The country had to break free from irredentist claims (that is, claims based on a historical or cultural tie) by Morocco to the entire nation. Morocco did not officially recognize Mauritania's independence until 1969, and the Moroccan claim to Mauritania contributed to the complicated Western

Sahara dispute of the 1970s. More recently, internal conflicts between the country's Maure and black African populations have led to international problems with Senegal and other neighbors to the south.

THE DESERT WAR: CONFLICT AND RECONCILIATION

When Mauritania became independent in 1960, the Western Sahara was an occupied territory of Spain. But even then it was clear that Spain would have to abandon its claims to the Western Sahara, probably sooner rather than later. But what would happen to the territory after Spain withdrew? The government in Nouakchott was extremely suspicious of Morocco's intentions, even after that country finally recognized Mauritania as an independent country. Because of this, Mauritania did not want Morocco to take over the Western Sahara. This would make Morocco its neighbor, and might spark a renewed Moroccan interest in Mauritanian land. Instead, the Daddah government hoped the Western Sahara could be set up as a buffer state, which would either become an independent country or would be partially (or wholly) occupied by Mauritania. Either way, this would provide at least a measure of protection from Morocco and any historical claim that kingdom's armies might try to enforce.

Although the Daddah regime—as well as a large number of Mauritanians—supported the idea of an independent Western Sahara, by the mid-1970s it was clear this was not to be. When, in 1975, the International Court of Justice ruled that neither Morocco nor Mauritania was entitled to claim the territory, both nations decided to ignore this ruling. The two countries got together and came up with what would become known as the Madrid Agreements: Morocco would get the northern two-thirds of the Western Sahara, Mauritania the southern third. It was not a total victory, but without the agreements, the Daddah regime calculated, Morocco would simply have occupied the entire territory in question, and brought its borders closer to the heart of Mauritania.

What happened next, though, turned out to be a disaster for Mauritania. As soon as the Daddah regime inserted troops into the section of the Western Sahara granted to it by the Madrid Agreements, independence-minded guerillas living in the territory fought back. The guerillas became known as the Polisario Front

Refugee women prepare Polisario flags before a rally calling for the independence of the Western Sahara territory. The dispute over the Western Sahara caused the Mauritanian government to fall in 1978; although Mauritania would have preferred to see an independent Western Sahara, it remained neutral toward Morocco's claim to the territory. The issue was supposed to have been resolved by a referendum of the territory's inhabitants; however, this vote has been postponed many times, most recently in 2002.

(Polisario Front stands for Frente Popular para la Liberación de Saguia el Hamra y Rio de Oro). The Polisario was supported by the government of Algeria.

This resulted in a huge cost both in terms of men (the Mauritanian military was forced to almost sextuple in size, from 3,000 to 17,000 troops between 1975 and 1977) and money. Government expenditures increased by 64 percent during this time, and an unpopular tax was imposed on the Mauritanian people to help pay the cost. Yet at the same time, Mauritania became less secure: the country, with its long and unprotected borders was frequently raided by Polisario guerillas, who even attacked major towns—including Nouakchott, the capital, in June 1976 and July 1977. Eventually, this foreign adventure would prove so unpopular and costly that the Daddah regime would be overthrown in a bloodless coup by Colonel Mustapha Ould Salek on July 10, 1978.

One year later, Mauritania signed a peace agreement with the Polisario Front, in which it gave up its claim to the territory and recognized the Polisario Front as the legitimate government in Western Sahara. But in 1981 Morocco filled the vacuum left by the withdrawing Mauritanian forces, annexing the entire Western Sahara territory. Mauritania watched this maneuver uneasily, and broke off relations with Morocco, but it would maintain neutrality in the affair.

The status of Western Sahara has still not been resolved. Fighting between Moroccan troops and the Polisario Front guerillas continued until 1991, when a United Nations cease-fire went into effect. Under the U.N.-negotiated deal, in 1992 the people living in the Western Sahara territory were to participate in a referendum vote to decide whether to become independent or remain a territory of Morocco. However, the referendum has been postponed several times, most recently in 2002.

In the wake of the Desert War, Mauritania has attempted to

improve its relations with both Morocco and Algeria. Mauritania restored diplomatic relations with Morocco in 1985. In 1989, Mauritania joined Algeria, Morocco, Tunisia, and Libya to create the Arab Maghrib Union, an organization intended to promote regional relations. However, this organization has not been successful in meetings its goals because of disputes among its members—particularly Morocco and Algeria, because of the Western Sahara issue.

In 1999, relations between Mauritania and Algeria were strained because of Mauritania's full diplomatic recognition of Israel. Mauritania's recognition of Israel also created problems with Libya, which is located along the Mediterranean coast of North Africa to the east. Since the 1970s Libya's leader, Muammar al-Qaddafi, has taken a hard line against both Israel and the United States. Libya quickly severed diplomatic ties, as well as economic aid to Mauritania.

RELATIONS WITH OTHER AFRICAN NATIONS

During 1989, Mauritania was involved in a conflict with Senegal, its neighbor to the south, that nearly turned into a war. The problems began with a dispute over animal grazing rights, and grew into *pogroms* in both countries. In Senegal, blacks killed lighter-skinned Maures, while in Mauritania the Maures targeted black Africans. By April 1989 an estimated 70,000 black Mauritanians—accused by the government of being saboteurs or spies—had either fled south across the Senegal River to safety, or had been stripped of their citizenship and deported to Senegal. Mauritanian soldiers occupied the Senegal River Valley and subjected those blacks who remained to harsh repression.

In late 1989 and early 1990, black members of the Mauritanian military began to be arrested. More than 500 blacks were accused of planning a coup to overthrow the Taya government, and were executed.

The Organization of African Unity tried to mediate the dispute between Mauritania and Senegal in 1990, but failed. The tensions persisted—at one point the countries exchanged artillery fire over the border, and war seemed imminent. In the summer of 1991 Senegal's president, Abdou Diouf, worked with the Taya government on a peace agreement, which was signed July 18, 1991.

Although the Mauritania-Senegal border was reopened, and some of the refugees and exiles began to return to their homes in the river valley, many blacks remained in refugee camps in Senegal. Their property was confiscated by the government and sold to Maures. As of 2003, tens of thousands of the Mauritanian blacks were still living in refugee camps, hoping to one day return to Mauritania and recover their homes and belongings.

Tensions between Senegal and Mauritania flared again in 2000, when Senegal announced a plan to divert water from the Senegal River to irrigate its farmland. The Mauritanian government argued this would deprive its own farmers of water, and ordered Senegalese workers to be expelled from the country. However, this round of deportations was carried out without the violence that occurred in 1989–91, according to a United Nations report.

Mauritania has also attempted to maintain good relationships with its other African neighbors. During the 1990s, the country helped to repatriate refugees who had fled an ethnic conflict in Mali. In 1994 Mauritania signed an agreement to work with Mali and Senegal on the issue of border security. Enforcement of national boundaries is a tough challenge in this poor and sparsely populated part of the world, and the three nations pledged to stop the smuggling of weapons, drugs, and "extremism" over their borders. In 1998, Mauritania, Senegal, and Mali participated in French-sponsored military exercises intended to train peacekeeping forces in Africa.

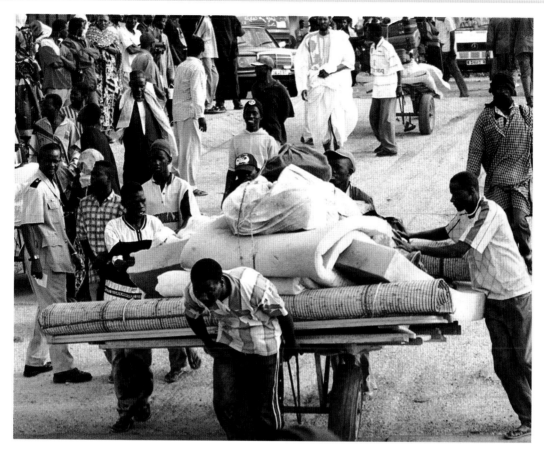

A Mauritanian pushes his belongings on a cart on his way to catch the ferry from Senegal to Rosso, Mauritania, June 2000. In that year Senegal and Mauritania each expelled thousands of the other country's nationals after a dispute over an irrigation project on the Senegal River. Though this incident was resolved without the two countries breaking off diplomatic relations, and without the violence that occurred during the 1989–91 dispute, it illustrates the tensions that remain between these neighbors today.

RELATIONS WITH THE WEST AND ISRAEL

Today, Mauritania enjoys "excellent" relations with the United States, according to the U.S. State Department. However, that was not always the case. Although in the early days after Mauritania's independence, the United States seemed to be cautiously optimistic about the new nation, relations between Nouakchott and

Washington ruptured in June 1967, during the Six-Day War between Israel and her Arab neighbors. (Mauritania, being an entirely Muslim and largely Arab state, supported the Arab forces that were attacked by Israel, while the United States was Israel's strongest supporter). Diplomatic relations were cut off between the Mauritanians and the United States, although two years later they were restored—despite continuing disagreement on the Israel-Palestine question.

In 1983, the U.S. Agency for International Development (USAID) began to provide financial assistance to Mauritania. Over the next eight years, USAID gave $67.3 million in development assistance. The United States also gave Mauritania tens of millions of dollars in emergency food assistance during the 1980s and early 1990s.

The next major breach in U.S./Mauritanian relations came in the late 1980s, during the forced deportation of tens of thousands of Mauritanians to Senegal. Things got worse when Mauritania voiced support for Iraqi dictator Saddam Hussein both before and during the 1991 Gulf War, and when the United States condemned human rights abuses by the Mauritanian military that same year.

After the U.S.-led coalition forces crushed Saddam Hussein's army, and the United States cut off of American economic and military assistance to Mauritania, the government in Nouakchott altered its postion substantially. Since 1991, relations between the United States and Mauritania have steadily improved. As a result, the U.S. has continued to provide aid.

Mauritania has even moderated its stance on Israel. Although much of the Arab world continues to oppose the existence of Israel, in 1995 Mauritania has established full diplomatic relations with the Jewish homeland. This is a step only two other Arab nations, Egypt and Jordan, have taken; two other nations of the Maghrib, Morocco and Tunisa, have established lower-level ties with Israel. Mauritania's moves were not entirely altruistic. Instead, the Taya government was motivated by political and economic factors—the country wanted to obtain Israeli expertise in such areas as agriculture and medicine, and to win credit in the West for its openness toward the Jewish state.

Some Mauritanian opposition parties have tried to use the Israel issue to their advantage. The Progressive People's Alliance recently called on Mauritanians to reject "the Zionist entity and all forms of relations with it," and to support "the Palestinian Intifada and Arab and Islamic peoples in order to resist the Zionist infiltration."

Mauritania also enjoys good relations with most European nations, including her former colonizer, France. Though the two countries were not close after Mauritania became independent, during the 1990s relations between Nouakchott and Paris finally thawed. In December 1993, President Taya held what were described as "fruitful" discussions with both French President François Mitterand and Prime Minister Edouard Balladur. Ties between the two nations were strengthened between 1997 and 1998, when the heads of state of France and Mauritania exchanged official visits and consolidated relations.

Outside of the Western world, one large country Mauritania has strong ties to is China. Since establishing relations in 1965, China and Mauritania have enjoyed a surprisingly close relationship. Mauritania supported China's entry into the World Trade Organization (WTO); in return, China has provided aid to Nouakchott while Chinese companies have contracted to help with agriculture and irrigation projects.

As the people of Mauritania attempt to build their relatively young country, much will depend on the direction its government decides to follow. The continued influence of the United States and the West may help Mauritania move closer to democracy and force the end of slavery. Although much work remains to be done, at this point in history Mauritania's future looks positive.

CHRONOLOGY

5,000 B.C.: Prehistoric rock paintings appear in the region we today call Mauritania, depicting a land teeming with wildlife.

A.D. 500: Kingdom of Ghana begins to emerge as a regional military and trading power.

570: Prophet Muhammad born in Mecca on the Arabian Peninsula.

622: Muhammad is chased out of Mecca and moves to Medina with his family and followers.

632: Muhammad dies.

642: Islam begins to sweep across North Africa.

739–740: Rebellion of North African "Kharijites" against the ruling caliphs of Islam.

1042: Jihad, or holy war, is declared by the Almoravids, who spread Islam through West Africa and into Spain.

1076: Koumbi Saleh is captured by Almoravid forces.

13th century: Sufism grows in popularity in the Mauritania region.

15th century: Portuguese explorers follow the coast of Africa south, stopping to establish trading posts in Mauritania and other areas.

1840: French settle in Senegal, and eventually extend their control into the neighboring areas, including Mauritania.

1904: France initiates a policy of "peaceful penetration"; gets local religious leaders to sign off on French control of the country.

1912: After "peaceful penetration" fails to do the job, French military might consolidates Mauritania.

1940: During World War II France falls to Germany in June; Mauritania becomes a possession of the collaborationist Vichy government.

1946: After a post-war conference, Mauritania is officially separated from Senegal.

1952: Mauritanian Entente Party easily wins control in the territorial assembly after running on a pro-independence platform.

1956: A "Council of Government" is formed to perform most administrative functions locally, rather than in Paris. The first government under this system convenes the following year, led by Moktar Ould Daddah.

CHRONOLOGY

1960: Mauritania officially declares independence, with Daddah at the helm, on November 28.

1960s: Weather patterns begin to change again in western Africa, leading to an expansion of the desert and long periods of drought.

1964: Mauritania declares an official one-party state in February.

1976: Mauritania and Morocco agree to divide the Spanish (Western) Sahara following Spain's withdrawal from the territory.

1978: After losses in the Western Sahara in June, Daddah is overthrown by Colonel Mustapha Ould Salek.

1979: Salek overthrown; after a plane crash kills one of the new leaders a month later, Colonel Mohamed Khouna Haidalla takes over power; Mauritania withdraws from its portion of the Western Sahara.

1984: Colonel Maaouya Ould Sid'Ahmed Taya takes advantage of an overseas trip by Haidalla to seize power.

1986: Popular vote in Nouakchott and the regional capitals elect members of their 13 municipal councils—Mauritania's first step toward democratic governing.

1989: The "Events of 1989" occur when a border skirmish with Senegal leads to tens of thousands of Mauritanians being forcibly deported across the Senegal River.

1991: A new Mauritanian constitution is approved.

1997: Taya is reelected as president with 91 percent of the vote.

2001: Construction begins on a 9-mile (14-km) road between Guergat, in southern Morocco, and Nouadhibou, in northern Mauritania.

2002: A total lack of rain between July and September leads to drought that damages crops and forces the country to seek international famine relief.

2003: The World Food Program launches a drought-relief program in Mauritania; in June army officers attempt to overthrow the Taya government, but the coup proves unsuccessful after two days of heavy fighting in Nouakchott.

2004: Locusts destroy approximately 40 percent of the crops grown in Mauritania; two more coup attempts fail in August and September.

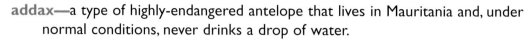

addax—a type of highly-endangered antelope that lives in Mauritania and, under normal conditions, never drinks a drop of water.

adherent—someone who follows a particular religion, cause, or leader.

Almoravids—an austere Islamic sect that brought about the downfall of the Kingdom of Ghana and established its rule throughout much of the Maghrib.

amir—Arabic word for tribal or religious chieftain.

Berbers—early inhabitants of North Africa; in Mauritania, they were nomadic tribesmen.

bicameral—used to describe a lawmaking assembly with two separate and distinct houses, or groups of lawmakers.

Kabba—sacred stone in Mecca toward which Muslims pray.

Qur'an—the Muslim holy book; dictated by the prophet Muhammad in the seventh century A.D.; also spelled Koran.

Maghrib—region of northwestern Africa that includes Algeria, Morocco, Tunisia, and Mauritania.

marabout—a highly respected religious leader, or teacher, in Islam whose influence extends beyond religion into all forms of Mauritanian life, especially politics.

matrilineal—inherited or traced through the female side of a family.

Maures (Moors)—the descendants of Berbers and Arabs, who speak the Hassaniya dialect of Arabic. Maures form the ruling class of Mauritania.

medressas—Islamic schools that teach only the Qur'an and basic literacy, but which supplement the Mauritanian educational system.

monotheistic—used to describe religions that believe there is only one God. The world's major monotheistic religions include Judaism, Christianity, and Islam.

pogrom—a planned campaign of persecution or extermination directed against an ethnic group and sanctioned by the government.

polytheistic—used to describe religions in which multiple deities are worshipped.

privatize—to transfer ownership of a company or public utility from the state to a private individual, corporation, or organization.

GLOSSARY

probity—absolute moral correctness.

reg—flat, uninhabited desert plains that stretch from Algeria into eastern Mauritania.

Sahel—a name given to the region between the coast of west Africa and the Sahara Desert. *Sahel* is an Arabic word for "shore"; the region was considered the southern shore of the Sahara, which was often compared to a sea.

Sharia—a civil legal code based on the Qur'an.

theocratic—used to describe government by religious leaders.

tribute—a payment made by one ruler or state to another as a sign of submission.

FURTHER READING

Celati, Gianni. *Adventures in Africa*. Chicago: Chicago University Press, 2000.

Connah, Graham. *African Civilizations: Pre-colonial Cities and States in Tropical Africa*. Cambridge: Cambridge University Press, 1987.

Damis, John. *Conflict in Northwest Africa: The Western Sahara Dispute*. Washington: Hoover Institute Press, 1983.

DeVillers, Marq, and Sheila Hirtle. *Sahara: A Natural History*. New York: Walker and Company, 2002.

Diallo, Garba. *Mauritania: The Other Apartheid?* Uppsala: Nordic Africa Institute Press, 1993.

Goodsmith, Lauren. *The Children of Mauritania: Days in the Desert and at the River Shore*. Minneapolis: Carolrhoda Books, 1997.

Grove, A.T. *The Changing Geography of Africa*. 2nd ed. Oxford: Oxford University Press, 1994.

Lamb, David. *The Africans: Encounters from the Sudan to the Cape*. New York: Random House, 1992.

Langeweische, William. *Sahara Unveiled: A Journey Across the Desert*. New York: Vintage Press, 1997.

INTERNET RESOURCES

www.mauritaniapost.com

News about Mauritania from local sources and news outlets around the world.

www.allafrica.com/mauritania

News from Mauritania, updated sporadically is available on AllAfrica.com.

http://lexicorient.com/m.s/mauritan/index.htm

An excellent and comprehensive tour around Mauritania.

http://i-cias.com/e.o/mauritan.htm

A good overview, with commentary, of issues concerning the land, politics, and people of Mauritania.

http://www.mauritaniembassy-usa.org/

The website of the Embassy of the Islamic Republic of Mauritania to the United States provides official information about Mauritania.

Numbers in **bold italic** refer to captions.

INDEX

PICTURE CREDITS

CONTRIBUTORS

The **Foreign Policy Research Institute (FPRI)** served as editorial consultants for the Modern Middle East Nations series. FPRI is one of the nation's oldest "think tanks." The Institute's Middle East Program focuses on Gulf security, monitors the Arab-Israeli peace process, and sponsors an annual conference for teachers on the Middle East, plus periodic briefings on key developments in the region.

Among the FPRI's trustees is a former Secretary of State and a former Secretary of the Navy (and among the FPRI's former trustees and interns, two current Undersecretaries of Defense), not to mention two university presidents emeritus, a foundation president, and several active or retired corporate CEOs.

The scholars of FPRI include a former aide to three U.S. Secretaries of State, a Pulitzer Prize–winning historian, a former president of Swarthmore College and a Bancroft Prize–winning historian, and two former staff members of the National Security Council. And the FPRI counts among its extended network of scholars—especially its Inter-University Study Groups—representatives of diverse disciplines, including political science, history, economics, law, management, religion, sociology, and psychology.

Dr. Harvey Sicherman is president and director of the Foreign Policy Research Institute in Philadelphia, Pennsylvania. He has extensive experience in writing, research, and analysis of U.S. foreign and national security policy, both in government and out. He served as Special Assistant to Secretary of State Alexander M. Haig Jr. and as a member of the Policy Planning Staff of Secretary of State James A. Baker III. Dr. Sicherman was also a consultant to Secretary of the Navy John F. Lehman Jr. (1982–1987) and Secretary of State George Shultz (1988).

A graduate of the University of Scranton (B.S., History, 1966), Dr. Sicherman earned his Ph.D. at the University of Pennsylvania (Political Science, 1971), where he received a Salvatori Fellowship. He is author or editor of numerous books and articles, including *America the Vulnerable: Our Military Problems and How to Fix Them* (FPRI, 2002) and *Palestinian Autonomy, Self-Government and Peace* (Westview Press, 1993). He edits *Peacefacts*, an FPRI bulletin that monitors the Arab-Israeli peace process.

From his first trip to Egypt as a high school student, **James Morrow** has been fascinated by the Arab world. In the years since, he has had numerous opportunities to study and write about the region, first as a student at Georgetown University's School of Foreign Service and later as a journalist writing for a wide range of publications, including *U.S. News & World Report*, *National Review*, and *The Australian*. He currently divides his time between Sydney, Australia, and New York City with his wife Claire (without whose research assistance this book would not have been possible) and their son, Nicholas.